Authentic Transparency
Shatoria Christian

©2021 All Rights Reserved.

ISBN: 9781637902035
Published by Lift Bridge Publishing
www.lbpub.com

From Shatoria:

To God, I have to say thank You for being my protector and my guide. As I write this book, you have kept me in true peace and to help me be myself and be free from all the things that I had to deal with in my life. As I take on every challenge that has been given to me, you have allowed each moment to be a course of learning to better me for today. You are always good to me and I am forever grateful and humble to be the vessel to tell this story and pray that it changes lives. Not for me, but for someone else who needs it and they need you.

Ron, my heart and my protector. There isn't much I can say to you or about you that you are not already aware of. I need the world to know that I am in love with the fact you love me no matter of my past and pain. You treat me like a queen and always reminding me that I am. I am grateful for your love during this time of starting a new business and writing this book. I have enjoyed life with you and to share moments of the unknown with you makes my heart jump for joy. Thank you for being an example and leading my heart when I'm all over the world. Thank you for leading our children and showing that life is full of love and surprises. Remember that life is what we make of it. I love the life we are making and I look forward to our future.

Jamorian & Janae, my joys of life. Parts of my heart. You both are joys like no other. You guys are the bright future that I pray will take the world by its head and do better than I did. I know you guys will do great things for the world and I can't wait to see what you both will do. I want you to grow up and know that you can do whatever you put your mind too. I have faith in you and your future and my biggest desire is that you stay strong, keep the faith, and know that you are worthy of everything you dream of.

Kim, Carlos, Devonne, Quantarra, Valerian, Tony, Tia, and Tamarra, thank you for being you. Thank you for your support. Each of you have a different place in my heart forever. You are not just my siblings, but my loves. I wish the best for each of you and can't wait to for you all to live out your purpose that you are called. I am here to cheer you on because I know there is greatness. Love you always.

Onisa, Brendaria, Natasha, Latasha, Amy, Angela, Sabrina, Medina, Dafeney, Tashi, and Nisha, I have no words to express my true gratitude for being my strong support system. Days to cry and be real. You hold me accountable and as my brother said at the wedding, you are parts of the bike Ron and I ride in our life. You all haven't judged and you have never second guessed my movements. Thank you for being the best of the best when it comes to friendship, and a strong sisterhood.

Spiritual parents: Michelle, Michael, Marcea, Archie, William C. (Pops), Pastor Carl & First Lady Lisa, Apostle Robert and First Lady Stella, and Pastor Demond & Pastor Portia: My words can't express my thankfulness for each of you and how you have poured into me in my years of growth. You have guided me in my walk, calling and even to guiding my heart and soul in the right direction. As a child who didn't trust or understand, I am thankful for your regenerate guidance as I'm still learning and growing. Forever humble and grateful for you always. Love you

Veverly & Delores: My mothers who I missed with my whole heart. As you are no longer here with me physically, you are forever in my heart. Forever grateful for the examples that you both have set for me in being the woman I am today. I pray that I keep growing to be a better woman, wife, and mother. As you have taught me that I will not always get it right, but I will and keep maintaining to better myself.

Lift Bridge Publishing & BAB: My editors and publishers who truly believed, walked with me, and loved me through this long process. You have kept me a float and kept me honest. Allowed me to use this time to dig deep and find me within the words. Always making sure that I didn't feel ashamed. I couldn't thank you enough and I'm so overwhelmed with the love and support you both have given me through crazy times. Thank you from the bottle of my heart. I am forever grateful to you and your work.

TABLE OF CONTENTS

Preface

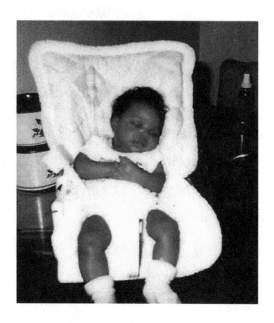

"You are made to walk through the storm."

Shatoria C

Being an authentic individual starts with being honest to yourself. Being something else can and will conceal what God has in store for you. I had a habit of trying to disguise my shame like Adam and Eve did when God called for them. Everyone has different situations that they go through that lead them to feel ashamed. For example, the way they grow up, not doing something a certain way, but for me it was putting myself out there with men and allowing myself to feel unappreciated. I blamed myself for all the things that happen to me, and it drove me crazy. The years of molestation, not feeling or receiving love from my mother, not knowing where and when I would eat, and so much more. My smile masked everything I was going through in order to make me feel better. It cost me a significant amount of pain over the growing years. They left me to fend for myself when I didn't have the tools needed to do so. I felt like they knew what was going on and turned a blind eye, but I wondered if they knew how to ask and received help in order to survive.

It is very difficult asking for help when I have watched young ladies struggle with being free because of the ways of society. I wanted the freedom that they had. The freedom allowed the ability to hold their head up and walk among people that talked about them. When they enter a room, they acted and carried themselves with pride by sitting at a table that others felt wasn't prepared for them. I needed that freedom that they exhibited. I want to speak my mind no matter what society would say. I wanted to rewrite what society felt was not of standards. I have seen my vision of freedom and that is wearing a pencil navy blue skit, a white button up blouse that is loose around the neck, and a pair of sexy navy heels that are about two to three-inch in height. Rocking my loose curls down my back and my makeup looking natural as if I was meant to shine.

Not caring what anyone else thought. At that very moment I feel a sense of love engulfing me that I never felt before. Society wants to take it all away. Society wants to destroy any and everything about how you feel about yourself. However, I had to learn to create the atmosphere and the feeling that I wanted to feel just by thinking positive thoughts. If I wasn't careful society would allow others to place me. With the help of society and people around me, I wrestled with my self-esteem for the longest as I wanted to be part of a world that I couldn't fit in. I was lying to myself about who I really was and I would think do they really know that I'm not happy with my current being? Did I really look good to others with the fake smile and the made-up goals? After a while, I had to learn that I needed to be worked on and that work came with God allowing me to be transparent and really seeing myself for once. Always checking myself before walking out a door, but standing in a mirror, I saw the faces of me and I didn't like what I was seeing. I needed a change and in order to have that type of freedom where I had my suit on with my heels and head held up high, I needed to be genuine. It was time to be transparent to others, but more so to myself.

The chains I carried of judgment, lies, and rejection were some of the hardest experiences I had to face. The process and growth over time appeared as I allowed myself to be seen in my true identity. None of it was in color, but black and white. It allowed me to see me for who I was becoming, who I am, and what I was leaving behind. Working to gain the best part of me required that I withstand a time where there was no strength or willpower. My journey into learning my identity and embracing the truth of my character wasn't a peaceful walk. During this journey, I will uncover the struggles of my life, which is the real side of myself. The combat to be comfortable in expressing my walk allowed me to lift my head high, face what society felt like was a success, and deal with my battle of forgiveness which held me back from moving forward. I challenged myself by facing things that continually tried to keep me at the bottom with no growth. Learning that my "L's" were lessons and not losses and its lesson learned to better myself. I hope as you read, my journey will inspire you to see the breakdown of my pain, suffering, and misinterpretation of life.

Becoming authentic and transparent has allowed me to grasp, teach, and love on those who are walking this same walk. I am still moving forward with my growth, but besides God, I thank my late mother and late grandmother for their teachings. They taught the decent, immoral, and foul of this painful world. Prepare yourself to be uncomfortable as it was uncomfortable for me to write the truth behind my pain. I am giving you access to a window view of my heart. Welcome to the authentic transparency of my transformation.

INTRODUCTION

The Order of Freedom

"I am beautiful."

Shatoria C

Spending many years trying to figure out myself to many people and the miserable part is I didn't know who I was. Faking the real me or just hiding behind the smile that can brighten up a room. Learning about me and who I was, was going to take time. I started going back to church in 2003 and I remember being taught faith. I can't believe that has been over 17 years ago. There are days where I need an extra boost and sometimes, I have to reach back to the old days when I first learned and embrace myself, my hurt, my pain, and just trying to grow mentally. Needing to be stimulated, valued, and loved, I went to my bookshelf and it was there where I left it. On the top shelf of a dusty bookcase is where God placed my old journal right in front of me. In this journal, I found old notes from the church I used to attend. In the pages of this journal, which was dated November 22, 2003, I found the words that I had so long closed off in my mind. I wrote a lot of notes without knowing how much I would need what was written in this book again right now. I started writing about sexual partners and how to be free from them, and throughout the journal my faith splashed all over each page. I even wrote the things I was standing in faith for like paying off my car, getting my first apartment, and promotion for work. Growing pains took me almost two years just to write things I was in faith for. Two years just to learn, embrace, and believe that I could and honestly to know that someone else believed in me.

There are moments in life when we need a reminder of how our transition starts. For me, it allowed my spirit to remain humble as I move forward within my growth. This journey also reminded me to go back to the unwritten words and thoughts that have plagued my mind and have had me trapped for many years. I was the kid who didn't have dreams of growing up being someone special or famous. I didn't grow up thinking of what I wanted to be or how I can change the world. The only thought I had was, fitting in. Please just let me fit in. Even at a young age, my self-esteem was as low as the milk left in the container that you see people put back in the refrigerator.

Many children have memories of baking cookies, having dinner together, and maybe riding their bikes with friends. My first decade of life wasn't any of these types of memories, and sincerely, there are moments I wish I could forget them. Most of those memories include my relationship with my mother and how that affected my intake of life and relationships with others. My mother was a woman who carried such a strong authority about her. She could command a room when she walked in like a commander of a military unit. She used her contagious smile and the sparkle in her eyes. Her eyes sparkled when the sun hit them and caused a glow of light. Almost like a flashlight being used in the dark. Such a beautiful site to see at such a young age. My mother wasn't a small woman but was built with a height of about 5'5 or 5'6 with what we call childbearing hips. Her hairstyle was that of jerry curl hair with the 80s style just like the movie Coming to America. I giggle a bit as I remember the sofa with those stains on them from the hair. When she was going out, I knew just by her scent, which was soft and lift in smell, that she had. I benefited from some of her beauty like her head shape, her eyes, her beautiful smile, and those hips. Just like her, I could get ahead to turn to look my way. My mother kept herself looking beautiful from her head to her toe. Her nails were done and she believed in her make-up. Her favorite color was red. as she sported her lipstick and nails in this bright color. The color of Red means power, and she carried that trait with a punch. Red was a beautiful color on her. She knew she was cute, and you weren't going to tell her otherwise. That's the self-esteem I desired and wanted. However, there was more to her smile that you couldn't see.

Behind that smile, beautiful scent, and sexy attire, my mother could be mean and hurtful. That sweet beautiful look also carried a harsh reality fearful nature that scared me. You can see the anger in her eyes as if they turned red to match her lipstick and fingernail polish. When she was mad, her voice was so harsh that her tone broke my soul. Her irritation would reveal itself by her biting her lip to keep her from saying something she may regret. That didn't stop her it gave her time to craft though as she said what she felt and she said a lot over my younger years. I actually could see veins popping from her forehead, and that showed that she was more than angry. I learned over time when to distance myself. Sometimes staying away caused more pain physically or mentally. Seeing that she had so much love for herself, I couldn't understand why she had so much hate within her. Or as I saw it and took it in, I felt like she detested her daughter. Growing up I have learned she didn't love herself. She could not love those around her and even herself. My mother lacked faith in herself, her thoughts, her heart, and her soul. She had a darkness that was made up of past issues about her that dominated the life that she wanted, so she never gained an accurate description of who she was.

My mother flourished as she appeared to have no worries in life, but deep down she was divorced, a widow, and a single mother of four girls. I accepted some of her faults as my own. Because of how she viewed herself, she turned to drugs and sex to take away the pain of being alone and right. One of her weaknesses was feeling rejected as in need to have someone for her and with her. She didn't know how to love herself the way she longed for others to do. When they didn't love her the way she felt she deserved, she turned more to the things that were hurting her physically. She had friends and lovers, but much of her faith was also into the drugs and sex that gave her temporary comfort.

Through all the pain and the hurt that she carried and caused, she was my mother. The type of pain I wouldn't wish on anyone, but how do you tell your mother that she is mean and hurting you? I had a true fear of my mother, especially when she would call me. I would flinch..........as I would flinch when she would tell me to come here. I was curious about what I have done when she called my name. Even today, as sad as it might seem, I still do this as an adult when anyone calls my name or say they need me.

When she wanted to chat, it was like waiting on the whooping that you were told you were going to receive hours prior. The wait was powerful as it produced more fear in my heart. Her battles became my battles., and She had many she was fighting. I wasn't able to help her, which became my failure in my life. I have a habit of trying to help people all the time, and this time was her, and I couldn't help her. I had to learn that those battles were between her and God. As a child, I watched her go through her battles even when I didn't understand what she was battling. I worked to always love her through the hurt and pain that I endured to never let her go. Growing up as her child, I sometimes felt like I was in the shadow and becoming her. I was a kid who knew didn't know anything. By the age of ten, I couldn't read or do math well and my mother was over me with negative words. I wasn't smart and maybe a slow learner in her eyes. I don't know what it was, but I felt like she hated me. All I could do was watch her and cry. I wanted to save her, but I had no life jacket for her. She was my lifejacket, at that age I felt I had no one else to lean on or love me. It came to a point in my life where I stopped looking for the lifejacket. If I was going to drown, then that is what will happen.

As an adult looking back, I have had many heartbreaks. I have caused my own heartbreaks and tears over the years. In reality, I am just like my mother. Not just in looks, but in my mindset. I found myself drowning in my sea of tears. Drugs never became my demon, but like my mother, sex did. I thought it would work and they would like me. but that was the storm of my life that I created and I had to face. I was becoming my mother, in which I understood her struggles. I started to treat myself the way others would treat me and I lost much respect for myself.

I learned better and started doing better at the beginning of the journey. My journey was just beginning and my life was in for a full rotation. This walk has been hard, and many days I just knew I would not make it. Parts of this walk for me was like walking on hot coals and just trying to make it from point A to B. One of the biggest lessons of my life is learning to forgive and forget. This was hard to do, but I needed healing. Healing from hurt and pain that was just haunting me.

Having that much hate was like not being able to breathe fresh air and just staying mad all the time. It hurt me physically, and that was taking a toll on my life. Forgiveness comes when you are ready to let go and be free from everything. Being free was important in my life, as it can cause more damage to the soul. I thought my forgiveness wouldn't come as I had many I had to forgive. I have endured years of heartache and pain that I wouldn't face. But it was time to comprehend the reality and my shame that I carried. I didn't know how I was going to walk this walk, but it is funny how God has a plan that isn't what you imagine. All I know was, it was time for me to heal because I couldn't take any more pain. It was time for the child in me to be put to rest. God answered my prayers, but not like I imagine. To be honest, I thought this would be a simple process, and I could release everything I hid inside but I needed to walk through my actual storm. Those drops of rain weren't it and weren't what He was referring to either. Being healed required for me to remember the memories that were holding me down by my arms, head, heart, and my soul. My healing wasn't something I was ready for, but the very thing I had to accomplish to be free.

Chapter One

Foundation

"Don't allow the small "you" to control the big "You.""

~Shatoria C

There are small things that excite me in my life, and being in school was one of those things. I enjoyed being around kids, playing, and just being free. The sound of kids laughing and yelling as they run around playing, was a different type of sound to a child who lived for those moments. I didn't have the life of a carefree child, but a life of worries and wonders. I share the excitement of starting a new journey is like beginning again.

Before COVID, I could watch my daughter, Janae, start kindergarten. That moment gave me such excitement, as she too was excited. Her excitement showed me she was ready to do bigger things and learn more. She is just like me, as she loves people but doesn't know how to separate the people that care and those who don't. Today, I want her to embrace the positive, and that day of starting kindergarten was a big day for her. Her smile and joy took me back to the memory of when I was her age and the way I saw the world. Her vision of it and mine was different, and so were our days of kindergarten.

My days at five and six weren't as grand or even peaceful like they are now for my children. Having many bad days are the reasons I take pleasure in my kids enjoying days like this. I remembered my time in Kindergarten as it wasn't all good memories, but even then, I try to rekindle the positive. Looking at Janae, I see myself in her and not just in emotions, but looks. I was this skinny and very tiny little girl as my weight wasn't much even for my age. I had a head full of hair that was in many ponytails with a big forehead. I promise you my forehand was the size of the state of Texas. I had hair that was thick and long and because my mom had put a relaxer in my hair, my hair sometimes was silky with curls. I used to love the ponytails with curls because that means it was a special day like school photos. A happy kid with missing front teeth, you would catch me smiling and as a beautiful black girl with slanted dark brown eyes. Like my daughter, I talked a lot, but very sensitive to things even as an adult. My entire life, I have worn my heart on my shoulders and I cared for people. But I was a kid. What did I know?

My first elementary school was North Avenue Elementary. Located in an area right outside of Atlanta, Georgia. The building was a big, brown, and reddish brick building that looked vintage. With so many classrooms and floor levels, it reminded me of the high school just with no lockers. The building had about four to five floors. I remember the gym, which was located in the basement of the school. In front of the school was one of the busiest streets I can remember ever seeing as a child. Traffic was never-ending, and I had to use this street many times to get home with my younger sister.

School was an escape where I could be free from things negative at home. I hated missing days of school because I depended on my safe place. I found the playground to be a cool, fun, and safe place for me to be free. The playground is almost any kid's favorite place at school. A tall fence surrounded the school playground and covered an enormous area in the back of the school. This was my place of freedom for most of my days. Being free by laughing and playing tag with classmates. It was a place to be my 6-year-old self with no care in the world. But I had to deal with some of the kids who were mean with words. They carried a sense of meanness with a little rudeness in them. Being bullied was a norm for me and I became numb to it. I was so numb that sometimes I acted as if I didn't hear them talking about me.

I wanted to fit in, I wanted to hang out, but I wanted to just be accepted. I never understood what it was about me that just didn't allow people to be nice. Even at a young age, I wanted to be accepted, but I didn't know what I needed to do. I had no control over how my life was going, and I didn't know how to take rejection. Rejection was normal for me, but processing it wasn't something I knew how to do. I was only a small kid with no sense of knowing what I did that was so wrong to be mistreated in such a matter. Playing with the kids but being laughed at at the same time was hurtful and confusing at the same time.

One of my painful days was a day that sent me home crying. My mother picked me up from school, which wasn't often. I was out playing on the school playground and rocking my favorite sweater and jeans, I was having the greatest time on the merry-go-round. I asked a little girl to spin me again, and she said no as she turned her nose up at me. I didn't understand why she just did it for me and another kid, but that kid jumped off as well. She yelled and pointed at me as she yelled I stink. She said it so loud the whole playground saw and heard it. The other kids on the playground laughed and point while calling me names. I even had some kids come and sniff me. I felt like a wet dog and there was no place to run and hide.

This is one of my embarrassing moments and the start of the downfall of my self-worth. I became humiliated, annoyed, afraid, and self-conscience. This day of being picked on was different, and as usual, I would hold it in. I didn't think it was my fault because I was playing and having fun until the girl decided she wouldn't push me anymore. My mother, on the other hand, saw it differently. My home life was poor already for so many reasons. Never understood why at that age, but I knew we didn't always have what others did. Like running water or food sometimes. When the kids talked about me, these things ran throughout my mind, but I would laugh it off to cover the pain and the tears. When I felt my eyes sweating, I would need to find a place to hide so no one will see me. The little girl and other kids kept teasing me, and they didn't want me to touch any equipment on the playground. They kept teasing but I kept on smiling and laughing with them. One girl even asked me why I was laughing and I couldn't answer the question. I had an answer, but I wasn't about to tell them my feelings were hurt. I needed to get away and since they didn't want me on the other playground equipment, I just said I needed to rest. I went and sat on the bench that was under an old pine tree. The tree had a strong smell to it, which was nothing but a pine tree smell. I've watched everyone play, laugh, and kept playing as nothing happen. They didn't see me sitting on the bench. I became a memory to them. I worked hard to hide the tears, but they came and they were heavy. The river was flowing and now I felt bad because I really couldn't let them see me cry. I used my sleeves from my sweater to clean my face. I had to do it quickly before they came to pick on me some more.

I was sitting in feelings of being alone and outside the kids, the other person I didn't want to see was my mother as she doesn't believe in crying or showing your feelings. This was a sign of weakness, and even at six years old, I had to be a big girl. My mother thought girls-controlled things around them. We are powerful beings, but I didn't control what was going on at home, so how was I going to control my feelings? I sat by myself for a short while, but it seemed like forever. Minutes later, I looked up and saw my mother walking over. I made sure my face was cleaned before she walked over to ask me anything. I didn't have more of a negative day as I was already there. At least the teachers were sympathetic and made me feel somewhat safe. As she walked over, she seemed okay, but my mother's life was a full plate and I was too young to understand anything about it. As she walked over, she seemed okay, but I was afraid of what she might do or say. I told her what happened, and she became a drill sergeant. She asked many questions that I couldn't answer and honestly didn't want to. My mother's concept of feeling sorry for yourself was "suck it up butter cup". For her, crying was weak and she didn't care about your age. Having a weakness wasn't ladylike. After she got on me, it was time to go. She seemed like she was tolerable because at least she didn't act out. Walking home with her seemed to be the longest walk home ever, and my mother made me remember that whining wasn't something we did. Walking home, I even smelled myself because I wanted to know. I didn't like the way I smelled or looked, but what was I going to do?

As we started getting closer to home, I see our apartments. Our apartments were the same name as my school. Funny how all the places I step foot in were all named the same thing back then. The apartments look like they were made from the same bricks the school was. We had a two-bedroom which may have been at the most a thousand square feet, not including the small two-step porch that was in the front. By the time we were home, my mother hasn't stopped roaring since we left the school, and it took a lot for me not to cry. Her words were harsh and were stabbing my soul. She was saying things like we are not weak and to stop crying all the time when I get picked on. Some of her words she liked the most were weak, slow, stupid, whining. I just wanted it to end and be over. She finally lifted off the harshness as we climb the concrete steps to our apartment door. The door was a clear storm door with glass, but it had black bars that covered it along with the windows of the apartment. It looked like a prison and felt that way some of the time. Walking into the place I called home, made me feel like it shut me off from the world. I walked into the house before my mother and all I could hear was a boom and a click. That was the sound of the door closing and locking on my innocence and embodying my fear for life outside of those walls. Walls I one day will break down. That was a promise to myself.

My mother made me go to my room and sit as punishment. Yes, punishment because I cried, because I told her what happened, and the fact she felt this is part of life and growing up. But importantly, she didn't want to be bothered. As long as my siblings and I were out of sight and out of mind, nothing else matters. I push aside my thoughts at the sound of the door opening and shutting and when it shuts the sound is harsh and loud. This was my life and felt like it was the Groundhog Day movie. This is when the actor relived the same day over and over and it seemed like it was never going to end. I just wanted to have a good day where no one is mean and or rude, but just a good day. I waited every day for tomorrow. I wanted tomorrow to be new, but tomorrow came and it was the same as yesterday. My one wish that I had was that tomorrow would be the beginning. The beginnings of new things.

"In the beginning was the Word, and the Word was with God, and the Word was God,

- John 1:1 KJV

Chapter Two

A Child's Fear

"Her scars were invisible to the world as they were hidden within her smile."

~ Shatoria C.

A home should be filled with love, laughter, and joy. But when a home filled is filled with fear and pain, it can weigh on a child and become a heavy burden. Children look for things that are simple and safe. A place where they are supposed to make memories and where they should feel the love and trust of those around them. But many children missed these moments and I am no exception to this. This isn't normal for any child's life, but unfortunately fear became a normal part of my life.

My fear started in our apartments. The bars that covered every door and window and even down to the brick wall that held the building up helped enclosed every fear and demon that enters. This child's fear was birthed right here in this place. One thing is that children can notice changes in their life, and the biggest event that caused the long years of heartache was my mother's late father's death. He was coming by to visit us and would have teddy bears and toys to give us. He started my joy of teddy bears and till this day; I love stuffed animals. But that all changed upon his death. I didn't know about death, but I knew with his death, he stopped with the toys and we didn't see him anymore. His death was in 1989 and memories turned dark after this and they flowed like a scary movie. I can still feel the discomfort of our apartment upon his death. His death was the first death I've experienced in my life. The aftermath of his death was felt, physically and mentally. That type of pain made me hate the life that was about to be my new normal.

My mother loved men, and the love she had for her father was noticeable. All I knew was my grandparents divorced when my mother was young. When her father left this earth, she became this little girl who was lost and needed a father's hug. Her heart became bitter towards the world as she didn't know how to handle her new normal. His death not only affected her life but those around her who had no control of their own. I don't know much about my mother's childhood, as we talked little of it. I had nothing to base her hurt off on besides the fact that she missed her father. I don't know if she knew the pain, but the pain was felt. Her pain became my physical and emotional abuse that was endured. When everything came to a boil my mother's rage would consume her and anger would take over. It wasn't just a belt or a switch, but whatever she had in her hand or could get too quickly. This became normal to me and fear became part of my life.

There is always talk about how children should be disciplined, but I received either a spanking or beatings. Her beatings were her allowing her angry out and trying to break away from her pain. It was like if she beat more, she could be free, but at the same time, we were becoming prisoners to her fear with no release date. She couldn't take it out on the person who hurt her, so I was easy to access to somewhat of a relief. She was jailed by her mind and this jail I couldn't help her escape from, because I wasn't equipped for the task at hand.

She had her moments and would try to make wonderful memories as she could. One memory was having my birthday in this small and cramp apartment with my cousins and siblings. Even though the apartment was small the furniture made it even more cramp. There was a dining room table that almost reminds me of a card table you played games on. We played spades there and yes; we were learning how to play the game at a very young age. We had the old school brown couch that was covered with neon color stripes. The couch was made of that itchy wool fabric There was also a brown box television with four little legs and it sat in the corner of the living room by the couch. It looked so heavy to me and it wasn't going to be moved from that one spot. There were some good days, but the bad days outweighed our good ones. My mother's hurt helped grow the fear that embodied our home and hearts.

I remember being scared a lot, and behind the smile were so many unhappy days. If the walls could talk, they would tell you everything it saw that came through those doors. I can't call it home because a home is supposed to feel welcoming and safe. My mother and siblings were the only people living in the apartment, but we had many visitors. There was hate, pain, anger, hurt, heartache, and death. They would come and take up space in our home and they became comfortable. But they also brought along yelling, name-calling, men, sex, and parties. Those walls were thick with the knowledge and information of what was within each person who stepped foot into its territory. Even with the sun shining bright, there were small peeks of brightness, still not enough to cover the ugliness that lingered within. The place seemed so surreal as an adult compared to a child. When I remanence of the apartments, I remember the hell that came with it. Have you ever walked through a place and didn't want to touch anything? That was me in my memory and looking in disbelief. It's the place where many memories become dark scary like watching the movie Nightmare on Elm Street. Thinking of the moment of wanting to wake up from this dream but you can't because this is the life that is before you and you can't change anything about it.

Our two-bedroom apartment wasn't made for a family of five to live in. Even with us living there, it felt creepy and cramped. My mother was trying to figure out who she was and when it didn't go right, there are chains of events that flowed and had a very lasting effect. Not just physically, but mentally. As my mind wonders in memory of the things throughout the apartment, I remember the one time her rage took another turn. Her facial expression is forever embedded in me of that day. The thing every kid never wants to see and that is their parents having sex and what did I do? Walk-in on my mom having sex with a man. My sister's nose bleed is the only reason I even went to my mother's room. After running back to my room, I sat on my bed scared because I saw my mother's angry vain. That vain nurses look for when they are taking blood. I was going to feel her pain, hurt, and embarrassment that day. All because she said I didn't knock before opening the door. I remember knocking and I thought she said what, so I opened the door. My mom had on this light blue dress and was on top. I froze in time for a few seconds, taking in what I had seen.

Before my mother came to the room I could hear her and the man talking. I remember him saying something smart to my mom. Like she didn't have control over us or something. If she did, then I wouldn't have walked in on them. She needed control and for him to say what he did showed her she didn't have it. Because of me, he left as I was told. She came into our room, which had two twin-size beds with a brown, five-drawer rectangle dresser in the middle of them. I remember seeing the belt in her hand and she went swinging. I was beaten with the buckle part of a belt. That metal part hurt and sting my entire body. My legs and hands hurt from trying to block the hits. Everything hurt because it seemed like every part of my whole body was hit. That little girl with the big smile and missing teeth was in pain and emotionally hurt. Not from kids picking on me, but being the reason to cause my mother to feel the rejection she felt when she was told she was a bitch or a hoe who can't control her kids. I thought I knocked on the door. The hits felt like lightning bolts striking my body. It wasn't the hits from the belt, but the anger that came with the hits. The physical pain lingered for a while, but the mental pain lasted years, which flowed into decades.

I've grown used to the physical pain. Communications was never a two-way street with her. It was she spoke and I listen and obey. Nothing less than that. I was talked to as if I had no value. I had a name that she had given me but wasn't enough for her to cherish. Children shouldn't live in the fear of not knowing if they are or will be covered with the simplest things of life like love, care, and protection. Love is the main thing children need in their life. A child should know and feel the love from those around them and know they are protected. That feeling of a child feeling protected is as important as giving a child food and water to survive. Children are innocent and are always trying to fix what they think they broke. There were moments I would say I'm sorry and it just wasn't enough. I felt like I wasn't enough. I learned that my mother was truly an enemy to me. She didn't love me because if she did, these things shouldn't be this way and I wouldn't feel trap in jail of uncertainty.

As a mother, I've learned to work with my children. They go through pain, peer pressure, and emotions every day from the world. I don't want them to feel pain from me. I refuse to birth fear into them. I desire to teach and reach them differently as they are different children. Keeping an open conversation to understand their level of pain and issues. My objective for them to never feel the level of pain that I've endured. Being able to have a conversation and walking in love has shown me I can deal with them on a painless level. I can easily put myself in time-out to make sure that when I have to deal with whining, crying, having a bad day, or just need to vent, that I'm fully engaged with what is going on. I've learned to listen and to understand the emotions of my children. I had to learn this as parenting doesn't come with a guide. It came with progression over years of healing from my prison. A joy I have is that Janae has a habit of putting her nose to my nose, and I can see the light in her eyes when she does it. When I see her light, it reminds me of that same light in my eyes. A light that was once bright at that age, but deemed as the spirit of the child was taken away. My goal and promise to my children that they will never feel that pain, but most importantly is I will never install terror. A child's fear will not only damage their soul but the light that burns in their eyes.

"He will bless them that fear the Lord, both small and great"

- Psalms 115:13 KJV

Chapter Three

Fear Not

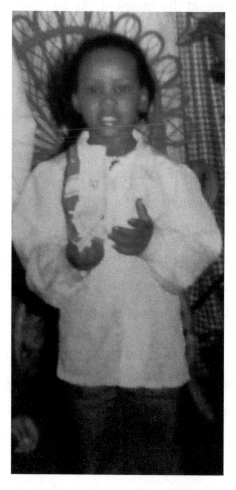

" I can do all things because I was created for this moment."

-Shatoria C

Music is something I find peace in. I love to hear the peacefulness of a voice singing. A way to express the feelings of either a broken heart or something that has given them joy. The poetic side of music reminds me of parts of the bible that spoke of the praise of David and how he praises and sings for God. I listen to music that flows with how I'm feeling at the moment. As an adult, I have found one of my peaceful areas in my home office. It's a place that is all for me and set up the way I wish. My space is peaceful and relaxing. With white furniture, the walls are painted black matted and accompanied by an accent white wall full of black written affirmations. There is a splash of gold color in this room that helps bring light to the space along with flowers on the coffee table that brings freshness. My cherry oak desk is painted white and completed with pictures of, my career, and family over the years. I love to sit at this desk and listen to music as it is healing to my soul. Jamming to my tunes like Anthony Brown and Kirk Franklin, Tamia and Snoh Aalegra. It all depends on my mood for the moment.

I was playing my music and getting work done, and one of my favorite old school gospel songs played. The song was called, Fear Not. I started to take in the memories when I heard it as this song was out in the early 90s and was the first gospel song I've heard in my life. I have an excellent memory of this song and what it means to me. I could do something for the first time that brought me joy and still do to this day. This song was the first song I have ever sung in a choir. I sang the song and remembered the first time I sang it. My thoughts took me back to the church where all of this took place. It was a small building with purple and golden-brown pews. This is where I found my favorite color, which is purple. The church was in a woody area that you could easily get lost in. It could hold about 75 to 100 people in the space. With church not being part of our routine, going to choir practice allowed time to learn about God and His word. I knew nothing about church or God and didn't know who and what the name Jesus was or meant. It was something about church and being around people that made me feel good. Could it be that in this place my mother didn't yell or scream at us? Maybe she found peace here as well. I was around other kids and I learned that singing was a craving for me. Singing was the food for my soul and I enjoyed and loved doing it all the time. I would sing and dance anywhere at any time and in those moments nothing else matters. I was ready to show my mom what I have been working on. We've been practicing for a while and I was ready. Deep down I was looking for something from my mother from this and that was having my feelings and concerns validated. I wanted to hear how proud of me she was and that I did a great job in things. This longing was deeply sewed into the brick of my life

I giggled a little as I remember the day getting ready to walk inside the church with my friends. We were getting ready to go and sing. We've been working hard perfecting each song. We practice this song and I knew I could do this. I looked around, and the church was filled with people. I was so excited like it was Christmas and I was about to open up my Christmas gift. As we got to the front the choir director placed us in our position, I started looking for my mother. We were standing in front of everyone with this pretty purple robe and I felt fancy. I finally saw her sitting in the front row and I saw something different about her. When I thought she caught my eye, I gave her the biggest smile from ear to ear with my missing teeth. I was ready, and I was going to give it all I had.

They gave us the cue and we started with our song. We sang as loud as we could, and our energy matched as we sing. This song was our moment, and we had a good time with it. My mom was smiling, and it gave me so much more energy. A moment I won't ever forget, and it was worth everything for my little heart to see my mother's smile. Besides us singing, another significant thing about today was that my mother was getting baptized. I didn't understand what being baptized meant or what it was, but it seemed to be a good thing because people in the church had so much excitement.

People starting to enter the church wearing white and everyone started shouting like we were at a game. I saw my mother's head was covered with some plastic bag. I had to think about it because I was confused about what was going on. I also remember being told you don't put plastic bags around your head, but what did I know. I was just seven. The pastor spoke and I was watching everyone. I still didn't know what they were doing and saying, but they seem like they were on another planet. I saw people before my mother getting into this pool and they did a prayer and went underwater for a quick second. When they came up, there was more yelling and screaming. It was finally my mother's turn, and the pastor said that everyone will be changed to someone new. I got excited because now I know my mom will be better. They said the water will wash all of her sins away and she will be better. Watching my mother get baptized showed me she was trying to do better and be better. Well, that is what I took from what the pastor said. I didn't know what the Bible meant, but I figured she came out clean. She was wet like when you have clothes in the washing machine, so she shouldn't be her old self anymore. Maybe my mother's new self will allow her to be nicer. I know today would be a great day since she is new, then we will start things anew as a family. Being excited about the day, I waited and waiting for my mother and to see what she thought about today. She hadn't spoken about how I did yet, and I figured it was coming because my mother was made new. Right?

After church was out, I hung out with other kids and acted as a kid should. It was so pretty outside and it was fun to play with the other children who didn't pick on me or make me cry. The laughter was back with no tears for once. After playing for a moment, I saw my mother coming. I saw her, and she didn't look happy at all. No smile and her eyes had no light that I saw in the others who went through what she did. I knew when she angry to stay out of way and don't ask questions. What I wanted and needed of that day didn't seem like it was going to come. I hoped that this day would be a good day. It started well, but it seemed like it would not end that way. She told me and my sisters to get into the van. We did as we were told and acted as if nothing has happened.

My feelings were hurt once again as I just didn't understand how she couldn't give an accolade of any kind. It was like pulling teeth to get a good compliment or something nice out of her. As we got into the van, my mother started her yelling. She didn't want to be talked to or touched by anyone. This is including the guy we were riding with. Whatever she was mad about had her over the top in her feelings. Maybe I was selfish because I just wanted to hear how I did. So, I put my big girl pants on and ask her how she thought I did. Big mistake on my part. She yelled at me to shut up and put my seatbelt on. She even threw in don't ask her anything. She and her friend went back to their fight, and I became tone-deaf. I couldn't hear anything. So, no one would see my tears, I not only put on my seatbelt, but I turned my head towards the window because I didn't need anyone to see my tears. I hurried to clean my face so she wouldn't see anything. I felt that I would never get a good job from my mom. As the van drove away from the church, I remember that this morning was one of our best mornings. I thought today was going to be great. I thought my mother changed when she came out of the water. My dreams didn't come true. Leaving the church, I notice that as we drove away, so did my good day. I watch the little, brown, wood church and full pine trees disappear as we drove off and that was the end. All I wanted on this day was just two words that are so simple. A good job is all I needed.

As an adult, I have learned that validation is part of the five love languages. Affirmation is a powerful part of who I am, and God had to remind me who I was and what I was to him. But it took me many years to get to that point. Learning how to love me and know that God has already told me He was proud of me and more. But at that moment as a child, I needed what I was missing, and I felt like that moment was my mother's love. That's what I wanted and what I needed at that moment. I remembered something the pastor said while we were in church and that was to fear not because God is with you. I grew up fearing life, but this reminds me, He is forever there. I learned that when my mother was baptized that her sins were washed away. With God's love, she was free, but she had to learn and know that she has a beautiful heart. It takes time, prayer, and trust with God. Outside of going to funerals, my mother didn't step foot back into a church after that. From that day, it took years for me to learn to fear not as God showed me to trust Him and to forever live in His peace.

"For I the Lord Thy God will hold thy right hand, saying unto thee, Fear not; I will help thee"

– Isaiah 41:13

Chapter Four

Seven

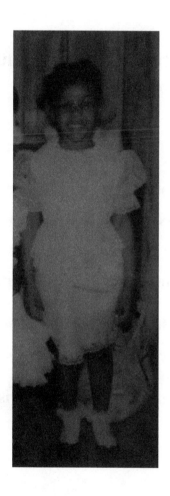

"I am more than enough!"

Shatoria C

Mature Content Warning

Please be advised that his section contains adult content.

If you are easily offended, have been a victim, or under the age of 16, please be advised that this can be a trigger. please go to the next chapter as this chapter is very detailed of a real event.

This chapter includes information of sexual and graphic content and violence.

Reader discretion is advised.

I watch my mother get dolled up by putting on make-up and getting dressed to go out. Men were always telling her she was beautiful, and she loved it. She was beautiful and glowed. She glowed like the moon at night over a river when she received affirmation from men. I can't count how many guys my mother had in her life, but one thing I knew was they had a sweet tooth for my mother and they all wanted a piece of her. I felt like my mother had a bank full of affirmation and should have been able to deposit some of that same love to me. I didn't know what she did, but I knew when they saw her, they loved her. I later learned it wasn't just what they saw, but what she gave. I learned at seven years old that the word pretty and other words of affirmation were powerful words to hear. It was a drug that was wanted later in my life, and not just by my mother. How can a seven-year-old be on drugs? It's easy when they don't know any better.

My mom had a "friend" who I will call "thief". He was a man that was kind of fat with a very round shape head. With his round head, he was slightly bald with this ugly mustache. It was thick, dark, messy looking, and covered up his top lip. He smelled like a summer sweat and thought he was the coolest man that enters the room. He had the weirdest walk as if he was walking side to side, just like a child taking their first steps. Besides the bad looks, he had a bad-looking truck. It was a brown truck that made the worst noise. Sounded like it was coughing every time he drove it. I hated to be around him and the word hate I don't use lightly. I was annoyed by him and very uncomfortable. Even his hello never sat well with me.

It was something about him and his presence that was sneaky. My mom liked him, but I think that's because he did whatever she wanted and or needed for the moment. My mom was going through a lot at the time as she was a widow and a single parent to four girls. She lost sight of things around her as she tried to keep it together. It was becoming clear that she couldn't handle things and became blind to the things around her. Like she didn't pay attention to the small things like us missing school, no food in the fridge, or forgetting that the lights needed to be paid, and my favorite thing was the fact I was writing on the walls in green crayon. She either didn't care or was blind and overlooked our pass time. Either way, her mental absence was impeding her vision.

The Thief was just that…. a whole thief. He stole things from people. He was greedy and was out for his benefit. "Thief" started my journey of selling my soul and I didn't know that my soul was being prostituted. He had no care in the world and he had to be in control. He was the male version of my mother and he was working to control everything, including her. He had my mother fooled because she could ask for anything and he would gladly make a deal, but I shortly found out that she didn't know her deal was with the devil. He had ways about him, and then there was so much about him. To start, I hated the way he would look at me. I couldn't do anything without him looking or even speaking to me. He would look at me as if I was a snack and then when he spoke it was a voice that gave me poisonous anxieties. The way our home was set up, you would have to go through the living room to get to the bathroom. So, when going to the bathroom it felt like a place full of mousetraps and you better walk carefully. My mom had a habit of telling us we had to say hello and give a hug. It didn't matter how uncomfortable it was, we had no choice.

Making my way to the bathroom and I saw the Thief and my mother. My mother indicated that it was bedtime and I needed to go put on my pajamas. I said yes ma'am and walk quickly back to my room. This walk felt like walking on hot coals. After changing, I went to say good night to my mother as this was a tradition. Giving my mother her good night, she seemed a bit out of it. Because he was there I had to hug him and say good night as well. He had this smile like it was his birthday and was enthusiastic about me hugging him. With his arms out, I could smell him and he smelled like a month worth of Georgia's summer heat and no shower. She told me again to hug him and I did because she didn't like to repeat herself. This is a thing I hate to do as an adult. I know where I got it from. Anyway, I gave him one, but it was like a church hug. The hug where you pat someone on the back and nothing but your hand touch their backs. Chills were going through my body, but I did as I was told and I did it quickly. I went back to my room with the white walls with green crayon writings. I finished getting ready for bed and once there, my sleep was for a short period.

I remember a tap on my shoulder and it was a heavy tap. I won't lie I thought it was one of my sisters saying they need to go to the restroom because walking through the dark in this house was just plain creepy. It wasn't one of my sisters; it was the Thief. When I think of that night, I think of the statement "the thief comes at night" and he did just that. He placed his hands over my mouth and told me not to say anything. I didn't know what was going on, but I didn't feel well. My life just flashed before my eyes. He told me to get up and I better not say a word. He led me to the bathroom and as we walked past the dark living room, I knew my mother was asleep in her room. I remember asking where my mother was. He told me don't worry about it. As we entered the bathroom, the room felt different. The bathroom had one sink with a rectangular mirror. I saw the bathroom as a different place at that moment. The bathroom was not this small, but at this moment, I felt like everything was close together and I couldn't move. With me and him in here was uncomfortable, and he was in my personal space. I couldn't breathe and I can feel every heartbeat as a lump in my throat.

As he closed the door behind us is when I felt the tears come. I was afraid as there were a lot of unknowns happening. Hearing and seeing him lock the door caused my flesh to become increasingly hot. It was like I was running a fever and shaking so much as if I had chills. My thoughts were, what was he doing or going to do? As I thought more the tears flowed more. This pissed him off so, he jacked me up and told me to be quiet. The way he spoke was like a common statement my mother use to always say. She would say it when we got a spanking: "Keep crying or I'm going to give you something to cry about."

So, you stop crying evening if it is for a moment. His voice became deep and harsh and I became tone-deaf because my voice and cries became louder in my head. As the tears kept flowing, I remember his heavy hand going up and down my face. The size of his hand reminded me of the Hunk. I was standing in front of the sink and the mirror and I saw my face with his hand. I had a tiny face so his hands seemed like they could cover my entire face. It was something I wish I could have not seen. I closed my eyes thinking this would help, but it scared me more because I didn't know what was next. He turned me around by my shoulders to face him. He wanted me to look him in his eyes. Even now, looking someone in their eyes is still something I work on. He stared me down while telling me I was so pretty and looked like my mom. He kept making this humming sound, and it sounded like a buzzing noise or as a bee sound. For a very long time, any buzzing noise I heard bothered my soul. He has a very nasty laugh and with that noise, I felt like we were in a movie that wouldn't end.

As I try to move his hands away from me, he moved his hands to my neck and whisper in my ear to never do it again. He even said that he would hurt me if I did it again. He asked did I understood, and I shook my head, yes, thinking he would just make whatever he is going to do quick. As our eyes matched each other's, I once again closed my slanted brown eyes because he kept looking me in my face. I felt something weird on my lips and as my frightening eyes open; his lips touched mine. Because I kept my lips tightly closed, he decided out of now where to push open my lips with his tongue. I felt his tongue, and it was nasty. His tongue was like a wet snake in my mouth that was trying to find a place to nest. I moved my face as

31

this was so weird. He was trying to kiss me like he kisses my mom. He could tell I didn't like it. In a smart-mouth tone, he said that I will learn and will get used to it sooner than later. The next thing I know was his hands going until he got down to my underwear. He rubbed my thighs and slowly moved to my vagina and I screamed in pain. With his quickness to shut me up, he had me thinking this wasn't new for him. As he quickly covered my mouth, my tears grew to be a flowing river. I liked nothing about this and it hurt like hell. He kept saying it would get easier as long as I am still and let it be. He was too comfortable because he sat down on the toilet seat while he unbuckled his pants and had demands. This had to be a nightmare and I wanted it to end.

My tears are still growing, and he doesn't care. He can't care how I'm feeling as he orders me to my knees and I remember his hands in his pants, but all I saw was his belly. It was like a Santa belly. Just big, round, and had a lot of sweat on it. Being on my knees, I still refuse to look his way, but he made me watch by turning my face towards him. With a nasty-looking smirk, he pulled his penis out with one hand, and with the other hand, he grips my jaw to open my mouth. There was no sex talk, but I did learn that boys had a pee-pee. As I have never seen one before I didn't know what I was looking at or what the fuss was about. As I wasn't cooperating much, he grabs my face harder and told me to take it. I didn't know what he meant, but I know I had no time to figure it out. He said to treat it like a popsicle and patted me on my head as I did as I was told. What I remember was gagging and not doing much, but he warned me to not bit him.

That thought came across my mind though, but don't know how this would have ended. He had his hand on my head and was pulling my hair, yelling at me, and telling me what I needed to do. At one point I told him no and tried to move my face away. That didn't go over well as he reminded me that there was nothing I could do as if I said anything to my mother, she wouldn't believe me anyway. The sad part of this was I believe him. He kept saying how she loves him and that she would believe anything he said. She won't believe a lying daughter. He forced me to keep going and what I know was this was the most sickening feeling ever.

His whole being disturbed me. I don't know how much longer before I became numb and had no more tears to shed. After he was done with forcing me to give him oral sex, he became upset because I didn't know what I was doing. Go figure! He had me get up, and I thought I was good and this is over, but that wasn't the end as he was not done and had other plans. He slowly took off my nightgown. I held on to it tight, but he wasn't having any of that. I had to remind myself to do as he said, and this would soon be over. After my gown was off, he looked at me with that disgusting grin. He kept placing his hands over my face and telling me over and over that I was so pretty. I had ponytails in my hair and I was just a little girl. I had little girl body parts and didn't understand what I could do for him. As he kept touching, I remember him touching my chest as if I had something there. I wasn't developed yet, but he didn't care. You can tell by the light in his eyes that he got happy and starting talking to me as if he was talking to my mother. He starting saying things like he wanted to see how wet it was as he took off my underwear. I was lost as I knew nothing he spoke about. I was shaking so badly. I took a chance and said once again I just want to go to bed. He was getting irate with me. I wasn't cooperating because I didn't know. How could I? I'm not my mother and didn't know anything about what he was talking about. I'm only seven. But actually, what the hell did I just do to him? What was that? These are the things that cross my mind. This wasn't normal and I just wanted to go back to bed. I wasn't going to say anything to anyone. He wasn't listening. He wanted to do what he wanted to do.

After taking my underwear off, he had me lay on the floor and I begged him to just stop. I said again I would not say anything, but he gave me a smirk. He didn't like that I was begging and crying, I remember his hand slapping me across my face. He spoke in a tone that made me fear he would kill me. He ordered me to do as he said or there would be terrible consequences. I think being dead would have been better than this. I told myself this wasn't going to belong or bad, but I spoke too soon. He told me to calm down and I remember him saying daddy got you. I felt sick and wanted to throw up. I didn't know who to call or didn't know how to pray, but want I wanted at that moment was to be free. I figure to look right up and not in his eyes and when I looked up, I remember seeing the popcorn ceiling. That ugly white popcorn ceiling. It looked like it could fall on us at any time. I was hoping it would come crashing down and stab him. My cries got worse as I heard him pull down his pants and my knee-jerk reaction was to close my legs tight. I surely tried it and he decided to turn me over in the nastiest way possible. I hit my head on the bottom of the cabinets and it took everything in me not to scream or cry louder because I have had enough.

I wasn't a heavy child I weighed about 50-60 pounds. His heavy hand held my head to the floor and told me to shut up. His hand on my head hurt so much because he was pressing so hard on my face. I felt like he was about to crush my face, but he was crushing my soul. I didn't want to think of what was going on, so I looked at the floor in between closing my eyes. The floor had an ugly yellow color with some type of circle shape. I allowed my eyes to trace the circles as he enters me. That is the moment my soul left me. My eyes popped open and I let out a scream. I begged him to stop and I told him it hurt. I tried to move by crawling away and it seemed I made things worse. My head was almost at the doorknob and he snatches me so hard back to the floor. He held my head harder to the floor, and I felt like he had many hands because I felt he was pressing on all of my body as I laid flat on the floor. I can hear him moaning and he wasn't listening to me. He got rough with me and I can tell he was angry because each thrust got worse. With every thrust that he gave, it seemed like I was dying. He was enjoying himself and breathing hard. I could hear his moans and the words that he spoke. Saying things like you know I'm your daddy and you like this? When I asked again for him to stop, he would chant things like I know it feels good, and just relax. He put more pressure on my body. I could feel his sweat as it was dripping on me like running water. I felt nasty and still wanted to throw up and out of now where

I did. My face laid in my vomit and I had nothing else to give. No one to save me, and after all the tears had dried up, I then gave up. He wasn't done as he decided to move from my vagina to my butt. As he rearranges my position he placed his hands over my mouth and when he entered I screamed, but it was in his hands so no one could hear me. I remember kicking and screaming as this pain was tearing me apart. I screamed for him to stop and I begged. I can tell he released himself as he took a deep breath and got up.

When he was done, he got up to clean himself. He didn't check on me or asked how I was doing. I was in so much pain and I wanted to go back to my room to sleep. As he was leaving, he orders me to clean up all by myself. I remember cleaning and as I was cleaning I started to cry more as I noticed I had some light red blood in between my legs. Nothing heavy, but enough to scare me. I was hurting to the point that I couldn't clean myself properly. Because I didn't want more problems, I did as I was told. After a short while, he came back to make sure I cleaned up the bathroom and me. He told me to use the restroom, and I told him I couldn't. He forced me up and sat me down on the toilet. This pain was too much and to be held down like a toddler to use the bathroom was heartbreaking. As my body finally released itself, there was blood that came with it too. He saw the blood just like I did and he flinches a bit, but not enough to help me. He rushed me to put my clothes back on, and told me to go to bed, but not without reminding me I better not say anything. Like with all things, I did as I was told.

I walked to my room and it was like walking the green mile. I got in my bed that I shared with one of my sisters and I cried a silent cry. This night hunted me and I don't remember getting any sleep that night because I feared he would come back. I know when I got up the next day he wasn't there. My mother was in a good mood and I was limping. She asked me what was wrong and all I could hear was him telling me not to say anything and she wouldn't believe me. So, I told her I don't know. She didn't seem concerned or worried. It was like I was hoping she would ask something that would lead to the question, but that never came. This night became the first night, but it wasn't the last. This event went on for about a year and some change and more than what I can count. I wished there was someone who could save me, but I was scared to say anything as I didn't know what troubles would come from it.

After this frightful night, my days became long and my fear grew like a tree. Thief planted fear, hate, lack of trust, pain, and loss of self all in the first night. There was no heart, soul, or spirit to fight back. I accepted the fact that this would go on and I didn't disobey him anymore after that. This became a routine as I remember going to my room and getting into bed. I knew if he was there when I went to bed that he would come to see me in the night. His shadow wasn't small and couldn't be missed. I couldn't pretend I was sleeping or anything. This was our routine. Getting used to something that wasn't normal was confusing. I couldn't cry anymore, I had no more tears. I couldn't yell or scream. I had no voice but had more fear. The type of fear that left me cripple in trusting anyone. My bleeding became less and less and being numb became my drug. Every time he would have his way, I would look at that popcorn ceiling or that ugly floor with the circles.

That night was the alteration of my life. He fractured my soul at seven but planted so much discord lived in me and my spirit. He didn't care, and he had no heart either. He stole the part of my childhood that destroyed me growing into a woman. In my mind, life wasn't easy already, and now this. The hardest part of my life is knowing that he was my first for everything, but not my first love. That is a part of me as an adult that haunted me for years because when people talk about their first, I can't. My first isn't something I was proud of but became accustomed to. At seven you don't know life. What you know is playing with dolls and being with friends. At seven I knew fear, being scared, not being wanted, numb, and worthless. Over time with him, my heart became numb to love. Every night he never changed what he would say. He would always say I was pretty. He wanted to see me smile. I would because then he wouldn't get mad. The pain didn't hurt as much when I just did as I was told. This became my new normal in my life. I smiled but that meant nothing to me. But for him, it kept him happy.

After a while, the Thief disappeared from the picture, but he never left my spirit. I was married to the very thought and the fear that was installed in me. After that first night, I have not slept fully throughout a night since and this is as an adult. Usually, I have music or medicine, but no peace. He took so much from me like joy and just being a happy kid. It took me a lot of years to divorce his spirit from mine. My smile covered every scar, fear, and pain that was carried.

He had a firm hold as he took things I thought I couldn't get back. For years, there were nights I dreamed of him and the nightmare I couldn't escape. These moments were part of the ingredients to my downfall as I got older. My dreams became harsh, but my soul was long gone when it came to what I needed or deserved. The nights with him were like a night of drug injecting. I was a slave to him. I stayed a slaved for more years beyond him. Years I have slept with the television on because I needed the noise to not hear, but the light to see the shadows. The flow of years of not trusting men and always remembering to do as I was told. I didn't know what people could do so I did it no matter what.

As an adult, I battled this spirit for a long time. I had to find the courage to let this out and to be free from it. Allowing myself the courage to embark on a new journey. This man was a symbol of the devil and took what he felt he deserved. All I know was when he left our home, he didn't live too long after that. Thirty years later, I have no hate for him. I pray he got it right before he left this earth. I don't know how many other lives were destroyed because of him, but I know that I finally found my courage, my voice, my strength, my life, and my willpower to know my worth and that I am priceless.

"Weeping may endure for a night, but joy comes in the morning"

– Psalm 30:5 KJV

Chapter Five

I Said Yes

"Know Your Worth."

Shatoria C

By the age of nine, I've thought I've seen my fair share of neglect. But now we can add abandonment to it. My mother's life was all over the place and we were there for the ride. She had us living in shelters and at one point I remember going to New York. I don't know who we visited or why we went to New York, but we did. With all that was going on, this wasn't anything new in our life as we bounced from place to place to live and visit people. I think my mother's heart was in the right place to get right, but she had her issues she was dealing with. We would never understand it because we didn't understand her pain.

The time came when we moved again but this time we moved with family. My mother needed to go get herself together. We were told she was sick and was fighting to get better. As an adult, I understand her sickness, but at nine I couldn't tell the difference. Our family decided it would be better for us to stay with one of our aunts. She lived in a townhouse with her three male children and husband. Her townhouse was pink, but the other townhouses were different bright colors too. Like blue, purple, and green. They all had small, brown, tree branch-type fences along the front of them. They were clean and peaceful and not what we were used to. My aunt was so nice to take us in, even though the home became pretty cramped with people. She had a three-bedroom. My sisters and I shared one room and my cousins had the other room. It was cool staying with my aunt, but she didn't know the secrets I have hidden away in the back of my mind. One thing I never questioned was that she loved us and she gave us her time when she wasn't working. She made the effort. I also feel like deep down she wanted to have girls of her own because she would dress me and my sisters alike. Besides dressing like twins for school, she made sure our hair was done and we caught the bus for school. For once I didn't have to worry about what we going to eat and if we had running water. I had a place to stay, and she didn't play about school or even wasting food. I don't know if she figured what she signed up for as she and my mother were sisters. She wanted to help, but she didn't have all the details of the things that went on behind the doors of our home.

As time went on living with my aunt, my craving for validation didn't change. Now my aunt would say we were pretty and all and I loved it, but I can't tell you why it just didn't satisfy me at all. Besides thinking she was saying it because she wanted something, I think I was just stuck on what has already been told to me. I was waiting for a shoe to drop, to be hit, or to be called names. I was Tori, and I was worthless, stupid, and good for one thing. Between my mother and the Thief, I don't know who was the worst. I was living out the words that supposed to define me and I felt and acted like those words were who I was. I wasn't being taught anything different, so I thought. I think my aunt was great with showing love, but when you are condition one way, then you are connected until someone unplugs you. There isn't much help when you can't be honest about the position you are in.

Over time, I worked to keep a smile on my face, but there was so much fear in me that made me stay silent from the actual world. Being fearful of speaking the truth came with me freely trying to find what I needed. I needed to hear how beautiful and smart I was. These things came at a cost, and that is a check I couldn't cash. The atmosphere of my thoughts and feelings didn't change, which also didn't change the pain I carried. I was a blind child walking around in a world of blind adults.

Living with my aunt masked that pain and desire until one day there was a knock on my door of attention and I answered it. This started my train wreck of saying yes. The first time I said yes and how I felt about it. The guy was so cool and he was dreamy to the eyes. This is when I loved light skin or red-bone boys. He was skinny but had some small muscles on him. He always kept his hair cut and licking them lips like he was LL Cool J. He was cute, but not LL cute, but and he thought he was the best thing walking. Every time we saw each other, he always had on basketball shorts and tennis shoes to play ball. I felt like he was a normal kid, but just cute. He was funny because he was always cracking jokes on my cousins, but I love he kept us laughing. He was sweet on me, he was a teenager. Because he was cool with my cousins, he would always be at the house hanging out. It was normal to see him around and to hang out. In the small short time I stayed with my aunt, I spent a lot of time with this young man. Like all the kids would do things together. No matter what, we all spent time together as one big group, and then it changed.

He had a habit of telling me how beautiful and smart I was. He said one day that I would go far in life and do great things. I gushed and giggled just at the thought that he would say things to me. I loved to hear it because this is what I needed to hear. I fell for the words more than anything, and because of the words and my thought process, the innocent side of his words disappeared. I didn't feel uncomfortable with him and his words. They weren't forceful like it was with the Thief. For me, I felt he was being real. His words were like a comfy winter blanket during a winter storm. I felt so warm with his words. What did I know? I was a little nine-year-old girl with a head full of braids and beads. This was normal. This was my life and I thought this was how it was supposed to be.

Being comfortable with him allowed me to be comfortable with moving to new levels. We all usually hang out, but this day was different because our elementary school was selling candy. Usually, we go out as one big team, but the older kids felt it would be easier to get more money if we split up. Well, this young man felt it would be great if it is just me and him. No one said no or that they wanted to be on our team, so it was easy. We all made a return time and made plans of who was going where. After about a few mins of conversations, we all split up and went to sell candy. As we were walking, his talking became more than friendly. He said how pretty I was today. He said other things, but I heard I was really cute.

He said because he liked me, he wanted to kiss me. I was excited as I liked him too. He was cute and I felt he was nice. He asked me have I ever kissed before or been kissed? I lied and said no. I have, but it wasn't what I desired. He happily announced he could teach me. So, I was like yes, why not? So, there was this tree that hangs to the ground you can go under it and hide. He took me to this tree and I remember him placing his hands on my face and he kisses my lips like a peck on the cheek. That was weird, but I was going with the flow. He wanted to try it again and so I let him, but this time I felt his tongue invade my mouth, I reacted by flinching quickly and he reacted sufficiently nice. He told me its' cool and help calm me down. I was nervous because it is a real kiss and I liked him. I finally took some deep breaths and calmed down and we kissed. I don't know for how long but we did. But that wasn't the end of it.

I don't know how long it was, but I remember him saying he wanted to show me something. I didn't think he would show me his private part, but I accepted it. He asked me have I ever seen one and like before, I lied and said no. He was excited as he felt he was my first. In my head, he was as I didn't want to count the Thief. After he talked me into touch and squeezing it he asked me did I want to feel it on the inside of me? I said yes. He kept with you are cute and smart comments. He even threw in the, you are special to me line as well. I fell for it all and allowed him to do what he wanted to do. We had sex under the tree that day. It was springtime. I remember seeing the colorful flowers poking up under the tree coming through. Honestly, this was better than the experience I had before. I had no emotions. I didn't know what to do. I just went with the flow. It didn't last long, it seemed like it was over before it started. I got up and got dressed while he looked around to make sure no one was coming.

After all, was said and done, there were no tears, I felt nothing. No happiness and no fulfillment. I didn't know what to feel, I've never known what to do in these moments. The moments of giving myself to others, I knew in my heart, I would never get back. We went on our way to finished selling candy and acted as if nothing happened. Just like the Thief, he said not to say anything to anyone. I agreed and told him I wasn't because I didn't want anyone to get in trouble. We got back to the group and went on about our day by hanging out with everyone and never speaking of it. After this day, time went on as well and we still hung out and again acted as if nothing ever happens, but we never did anything again.

One reason we didn't because his words changed. He wasn't saying nice things anymore to me, but he was brushing me off. Remembering my cousin at one point telling him to be nice because he became a little rude. He started speaking about other girls and they would flirt when we were outside hanging out. He got one girl pregnant. Now that I can do the math as an adult, she was pregnant when I slept with him. There was that moment where I felt nothing likable about me. A child with grown-up thoughts. I knew what I saw and thought that was the right way to love someone. It was all a made-up dream. The reality was hurt, pain, abandonment, and no joy in sight. I was a child and didn't see what was real. Saying yes to someone who didn't care about me, and everything he said to me was a lie. Saying yes because I thought he meant what he said. My smile portrayed what was going on behind the glare of my eyes. Being in my feelings and it hurt. I knew if I told someone would get in trouble and I didn't want to get anyone in trouble.

Telling no one about who this guy was. He felt like he was teaching me about sex and kissing, but he wasn't my first. He did something I became use to and that was lying and breaking my heart. He gets a gold star for being my first real crush. Searching for the wrong things led me to freely give myself away, and it killed my heart again. When asked when I lost my virginity, I was nine because I did it voluntarily. Because he would say all the right things and he said things I heard men tell my mother, and even what the Thief would say to me, he became an easy person to say yes to. He wasn't the last person I said yes to, but he was the one that spoke to my broken heart and for a moment it felt whole. That was for a brief moment. My lesson with this was a yes can still lead to a broken heart, pain, hurt, and being left to be alone. That is exactly how I felt. I wonder what could have happened if I just didn't say yes.

"To the praise of the glory of His grace, wherein he hath made us accepted in the beloved"

– Ephesians 1:6 KJV

Chapter Six

McDaniel Street

"Speak up even if it hurts."

Shatoria C

I was tired of moving around and by the summer of 1992, we were doing it again. Another new place to stay, which means another new school. After living with my aunt, I went back to live with my mother, after getting her life together. I was over moving and over going to a new school. This new school turned into my fourth elementary school, and I was going into the fourth grade. Because it was summer, I had time to adjust to the new home that we were going to live in. I didn't keep friends as we didn't stay anywhere long enough to have them. This time I hoped that this would be a good move and the last.

The new house on McDaniel Street was different as we drove up to it. I noticed some differences in the home compared to the other places we have lived. It has a bigger backyard than all the other ones. That's cool because we could play somewhere other than the street or someone else's home. This home was on a busy street and there was so much surrounding it. It was a nice green color with the trim being white surrounded by an iron silver fence. The small space to park was right next to the house, and the fence covered this space as well. We had a small front porch with white columns. The porch was just a little bigger than the one at the apartments, the big difference is that it had a nice front yard and that had me excited. As we got out of the car, I looked around. This is new as I wasn't use to everything I was seeing and all of it was in one place. There was a church across the street and it was right in front of the house. So maybe we could go, and don't have to worry about a ride. To the right of the home was a nice corner store, and I see many people going in and out. It had a set of stairs next to it with a small little balcony. It was made up of red bricks and looked like a little brownstone you would only see in places like New York. It looked like someone lives there as you could see movement looking in the window. I hear my name called to come on, but I was taking in the new scene. As we walked towards the door, there was a small shopping section that was beyond our backyard. It looked like a laundry mat and a hair salon. Outside was very different from what we are used to. We never had this much at our fingertips to enjoy.

The home was nice but had two bedrooms, which means we are still sharing a space. We once again had actual furniture and I even have a bed. This was an enormous deal to my nine-year-old self. I had to tell myself that this could be very different for us and things were going to get better. Living in this home full of items for once was nice, and I was enjoying it. After we got settled in, my mother signed me up for dance class and cheer. I loved it! I was going every chance I could. It kept me busy, and I met many young girls as well. It was part of the Boys & Girls program. I found out that many of the girls were going to be attending the same school. I made connections and things were flowing so well. Mom was doing well, and we were doing good with school, dance, and cheer.

Starting school was not so bad, and we even went to the church across the street from time to time. I fell in love with the corner store people. The store served dill pickle and pig feet and I decided to try it. My love for both items was birth. This was normal, and this was the best time. My mother had a new friend, and he seemed like he was okay. He didn't bother me and allowed me to live like a kid. As time rolled, I remember things changed. We went from having all this light and shine in our home to dark days again. All was splendid, but as with everything before, this would be short-lived. The house wasn't always as clean, and I started to miss school again. My mother and her friend begin to be on the outs and fights begin to start in our home once again. As I meet some new people, mom allowed me to spend the night at their home. This young lady was so cool as we were in the same class and cheer together. She had smaller siblings as well. We wanted to do a sleepover and hang out, and we finally did. She lived around the corner, so it was easy to get to her home. We had a lot in common that we could speak on and things we wouldn't speak on, but it became very clear of the unspoken things the night of the sleepover.

I took one of my siblings with me, and we had a lot of fun. We had pizza and punch along with laughing and being kids all night long. Going to bed and waking up to her parents is a night I will never forget. I heard the scream that sounded like someone was dying. The scream was like you could feel it in your side when you are having side pains. I jumped up with the friend, and we were all nervous. The young girl's parents were fighting like dudes on the street, throwing punches. The mother was asking and begging for help in between each punch. You could hear each punch that she took, and it was to anywhere on her body. I couldn't help in any type of way, but we stayed in that room up and alert. After what seemed like forever, the screams died down and I remember my friend's door to her bedroom opening. Her dad told her that all her friends had to leave. My friend looked at me after her dad closed the door and I saw the fear in her eyes and her fear matched mine. She told me not to say anything to anyone about what I saw, and that is a promise I kept. I learned at an early age not to argue or fight, so I packed our items and we started walking home.

Leaving the house, it was still dark and, it was about six o'clock in the morning. Their home was set on a hill so we had to walk down long concrete stairs to the street. Before we were at the bottom of the steps we could hear my friend's, mom screaming and begging him to stop. I could hear her saying that she was sorry, and whatever she did she wouldn't do it again. He made it clear in his tone, his hits, and his words that she runs nothing and she needs to learn her place. At that moment, I just wanted to get home. I knew I would have to explain to my mother why we were home so early. As we kept walking down the hill the next thing I heard from that home was two gunshots. They sound like firecrackers going off; quick and loud. shots. To this day, I have never asked or questioned what went on in that home in our short walk down that hill. I learned over the years there are things to say and not to say. This was that moment where I was going to lie and told my sister the same thing too. We walked in the dark and even though it seemed like it was forever it was maybe ten minutes. When I think of what happened on that night and what could have happened to us, God kept us safe. Walking in the dark on the wrong side of town. Anything could have happened and or someone could have picked us up. What was on my mind was how

I was going to tell my mother why we are home so early. To my surprise, there was another surprise waiting on us when we enter the home.

Once we are inside the house, we notice that all the furniture was gone. In the living nothing but the television set on the floor. We go to our room and our beds are gone. The room is empty. What was left was my mother's bed, her dresser, her television in her room, and the television in the living room. I didn't get it or understand it. Fearing my mother's words and actions, I asked no questions. She didn't even bother asking me why we were home so early, so I figured she had other things on her mind.

For a while, our beds became the long rectangle swimming floats. They were yellow and blue, and they were flat on the floor. At least I didn't have to make up my bed. I can't say our life was normal because sleeping on the floor isn't normal. Missing days of school, because you have to help with your younger sibling, isn't normal either. Being a kid wasn't normal for me. My mother soon had me stop cheerleading and dance because I needed to be home. I wondered about the when, where, and what food we were going to eat again. Our kitchen in this house was smaller than the kitchen in the apartment. Our kitchen was dirty, had bugs, and lacked food and water. The government meals, like cheese and peanut butter are what we ate to get by along with noodles with hotdogs. The cheese didn't melt and the peanut butter had oil. At nine, I was jealous of other people and hated this life. As an adult, I actually can smile about it. I have come a long way. Growing up was a big factor in this for me.

I don't know if my mother hit rock bottom, but her temper and her mood changed. Anything can set her off and her anger and my fear finally came to heads that October. I don't know what pissed my mother off, but she was in a mood. She asked me a question., I should have known better but at that moment my little self-found a way out of the hell we were living in. She came out of the blue and asked me did I want to live with my grandparents? This is the one time I didn't think before I spoke and came out with a full yes. I couldn't believe I said yes, and I couldn't believe she asked me that. I've never thought about living with my grandparents, but it wasn't so bad living with my aunt. What could I lose by moving again? That pissed her off that she sent me to my room and I was punished later.

My mother cussed and fussed at me for the longest. Perhaps thinking I was abandoning her by leaving. She questioned me and made it seem like I was ungrateful. Reminding me that she was feeding me and giving me a place to stay. All I could see was her angry coming from her eyes and at that moment there was nothing else you could do or say. I regretted that moment of saying yes to moving for the longest time. The moment she asked was so quick that saying yes, I felt good saying it. I regretted saying yes because I felt like I disappointed my mother. She felt like I betrayed her and disagreed. I've never forgotten that conversation, never forgotten how I felt as it rolled off my lips, and never forgotten how my mother looked when I said it. She made sure that I regretted it.

My grandmother was speaking in codes when she called me for my tenth birthday. I remember her calling me to say happy birthday and saying she couldn't wait to see us for Thanksgiving. Going to your grandparents and being excited, knowing you can do whatever and get away with it. I learned later that my grandmother had other plans. and what I didn't know was that my time on McDaniel Street was coming to an end. The end came sooner than later and it came by adding another change to my life. I didn't know when and how all of this would end, but I needed it to end. This change was coming but this time this change was for the better of me.

"Then I commend mirth, because a man hath no better thing under the sun, than to eat and to drink, and to be merry: for that shall abide with him of his labour the days of his life, which God giveth him under the sun"

– Ecclesiastes 8:15 KJV

Chapter Seven

From the City to the Country

Begin Anywhere

Shatoria C.

"You are not going back to live with your mother. You are going to stay here with us!" The words of my grandmother ran into my soul. My grandmother was firm in her voice anytime she spoke. Now that I think about it, her voice seemed to always be that way. My grandmother was tall and skinny. If I had to guess, she was between 5'8 to 6' in height. When you look her in the face, you would see her crazy birthmark mole. It was weird and I use to hate it, but it was part of her. She had the most beautiful caramel skin tone, along with some of the softest hair I've seen or touched. She hated her hair as she would spend all Sunday morning curling it and by the time we left the house for the church, there were no curls. My grandmother would get in the car and breathe a bit and we would all start laughing at her. She would always say her hair makes her late. Her hair was a pretty dark brown and mixed with a light color gray. She would always say that she was smart and had a lot of wisdom, and she can prove it because of the gray in her hair. Little did she know she was about to get more wisdom taking with us.

My grandmother was not the one to hug you and tell you she loved you. That wasn't her thing. Her embrace for people and life was harsh. She was the mother of four children and the grandmother of nine. She was an empty nester, but now she and my grandfather were about to embark on raising children again. We weren't normal kids, but another generation. She made it seem so easy, and she would always say that parenting doesn't come with a handbook. I didn't know what that meant until I became a parent myself. That was almost 28 years ago, and I still remember how I felt at that moment.

My grandmother was so passionate about us, but you could tell it disappointed and hurt her about what was going on with my mother. I should have known that visiting my grandparents for Thanksgiving wouldn't be just a visit. More so since my mother not too long ask if I wanted to live with them. Now it seems like I will be, but for how long. I stayed with my aunt for a couple of months, and now this. Here we are again with another move, another school, and new people. The only difference is this town isn't what I am used to. It was small and about 2 hours outside of Atlanta, Georgia. I was used to the city and having things around me I could easily walk to, as my corner store. This town was nothing of a city as there was nothing in walking distance, back in the city I could walk to different places, but here nothing was close. My grandparents took pride in the new home we were living in as they built the home for themselves. They weren't expecting kids at all and well, here we are. This was evident, as this home wasn't that big at all. It was bigger than the apartment on North Avenue, and it had furniture. They built their little two-bedroom home in Greensboro, Georgia, for them when they got married in March 1992. The home was completed and they moved in by August 1992 with no expectation of anyone living with them.

Learning that I am now officially moved, I looked around at the details of everything around me. The street we lived on was narrow and all the other homes on the road were blood-related family. This was my grandfather's hometown, and it was just like him, silent and simple. I've never been around people who were family and were cool with everyone living on the same street. Adjusting to my new home, it was a cute little house that was sky-blue color trimmed in white. The garage didn't have a door to it, and the driveway was gravel. I can't walk to anything nearby besides a family member's home, but there was a cow pasture right in front of our home and all I could see were cows. Many times, visiting the zoo and see many animals, but never farm animals.

My grandfather was such a superhero. Just like my grandmother, he took us in and loved us. He was such a laid-back man. He was tall and skinny with salt and pepper hair and a mustache. When he walked, his steps were so light you couldn't hear when he came up the hallway. His walk was like his spirit, and everything about him was peaceful. He had no blood children of his own, but he adopted me and that was love for me. Even though he was a silent man with few words when he had something to say, he said it. He always wanted the best for me.

Not new to moving, but this atmosphere was new. Here there was nothing I knew outside of my siblings. With a home full of furniture and food it was a great feeling. I knew my grandmother wasn't about to let her babies go without. She didn't play that. I thought this was a dream, but it was a home that felt like a home that you see on the television. It felt that way because grandma added her touch to the home. She decorated everything about the house, including the formal living room and living room. She had plastic on the furniture in the regular living room with an old school glass coffee table. That table was older than me. Now that table is about

70 years old. I knew grandma was old school with the china cabinet with dishes in it; you know the dishes you can't eat on but pretty to look at. One thing I learned about my grandmother is that she was fancy. She was not afraid to speak her mind, but she cared for us. I felt that because she took us in to live with her, so once again my mother can get herself together.

I learned a lot with this move. Moving to this small town showed me things that I've never seen before, like how much land there is out there. I didn't know how refreshing it was to see so much land, trees, and to be able to play in a yard. This was new to me. Some things were new, like having water well that had a little roof on it like the house. I later found out that this was the place we pumped our water from. In the city there are sewers and in the country, there are wells for water. I was expecting a well tower you draw water from when she first told us about the well. I finally understood it later. But it was still weird to know that our water was coming from there. I had a short time to hurry and adjust to this new life before school started. I didn't feel like starting back over again. But grandma was going to help us get it together, and I prayed it stuck. I don't know how ready she was, but I hoped she was ready because my education level was about to be a surprise to her. We were starting our new school on that Tuesday, 1 December 1992. Got to get through the weekend and it seemed to be a long one and busy. This is because we didn't have anything with us to start school and it was Thanksgiving as well. My grandparents spent the weekend shopping for clothes, getting us beds, and doing hair to get ready for something new. My grandmother hasn't done this since her youngest daughter and that was over 20 years ago. With spending the weekend shopping, I learned how far things were. The nearest shopping area was such a long drive. Felt like we were forever driving to the mall and it was like 45 minutes. Still, I don't know anything about living in the country and not having a bus to ride.

I had thoughts that came to my head. What would they say about me? Could I make new friends? How long were we staying? I hope no one would laugh as I don't know how to read that well along with other things. This is not new for me starting a new school, but then again this is a new school in the country. This time, I just wanted things to be different and my grandmother seems to be on the same page as she expresses her feelings about it. We are kids, so this isn't our fault. My grandmother was clear that she had had enough of the mess my mother was doing. I asked if my mother is going to get better and my very blunt grandmother was clear as she spoke, "I hope so, so y'all can go back home to her." She was clear as she said how she was too old for this.

This was adding four more kids to a two-bedroom home in the middle of nowhere. This was shopping on Black Friday weekend to buy school items for kids who have nothing. We needed everything from underclothes to hair supplies. At that moment I didn't think that she didn't want us there, I think she was just over my mother and her ways. She had had enough, and she just wanted to see something different. I felt like she did, and all I've wanted was to feel like they wanted me. I felt like my mother was just out for herself because I didn't understand why and how she couldn't get better for her children. But at that moment, it didn't matter because now I'm surrounded by new everything. I should be a pro at this moving thing and shouldn't be nervous, but this is the norm for me. At least things will be different this time as I will eat before school, have my hair done, clothes are new, I smell clean, and lastly just like my aunt did me and my sister were semi-matching. This should be a good sign, so it's time to get ready for Tuesday. It couldn't come quick enough, but I was waiting on it like a child at Christmas. Something new that I kind of didn't look forward to, but scared to do so because I don't know what to expect. I expected that I was a scared ten-year-old kid. By this age. I've had too many life-changing events and hoped it could slow down for once. We were about to find out as Tuesday was coming.

"Behold, I will do a new thing; now it shall spring forth; shall ye not know it? I will even make a way in the wilderness, and rivers in the desert."

Isaiah 43:19 - KJV

Chapter Eight

New Everything

It's Okay to start again

Shatoria C.

Tuesday morning and here I am about to start new all over again. I was not ready to start another school, but praying that this was my last time. In the need of a pep talk before getting to this school. Something positive because I'm not used to an area like this. I had the hope method in my head. Hoping they didn't see me as a weird new kid and my goal is not to make a fool out of myself. This was a country town and I'm a city girl. I wanted to get through the process with all of my nerves still intact. Why was a ten-year-old having all these thoughts?

I guess when you have changed schools and lifestyles in a short amount of time; you wonder about what's next. Not knowing God at this point in my life, and I didn't know positivity either, I was channeling something and hoping for a wonderful first day. I made sure I would not be talked about the way I was before. I have showered, I have on clean clothes and my hair is cute and ready for today!!! I told myself this, and it was going to be a good day.

It was time to get our day started. Off to the new school we go! Climbing into my grandmother's four-door white Toyota and getting settled in. I've never seen a car with blue leather on the inside. She had rules of no eating or drinking in the car. We never broke that rule because we knew we would get in trouble. The drive seemed very slow and maybe it was my nerves, but I took the time to take in the view. There isn't much to see like it is in the city, but then again there is much to see when you need peace. I didn't learn the importance of this till later in my life. As we drove I notice it was winter and the trees had no leaves on them. It was cold and the breeze wasn't that heavy today. I wasn't paying close attention to where we were driving, but I notice my grandmother went a different way than what she did when we went shopping.

As we drove, she explained to us that there was a high school and middle school as one, one primary elementary school, and one elementary school. As she spoke, I noticed that the town looked clean and well put together. The city isn't like this at all. Trash everywhere and it seemed to never be cleaned. The way the country looked was almost like the person who has OCD and needed to make sure the house was clean. The town seems to be at a very slow pace. Cars are moving and when you see someone you know they were blowing their horn and waving. That was weird for me because people were saying hello and smiling. As we kept driving along, I also noticed there were no homeless people or a bridge where they slept. I wonder, did they have homeless people in this town? I know one thing for sure and that I wasn't used to this type of atmosphere.

After being in my thoughts for a moment, I came out of it as we pulled up to this long building that was made of bricks. It had a very long walkway to the front door from where my grandmother parked. Remembering my grandmother's voice being soft as she asked me was I ready, and her saying to me it will be okay. I don't know what gave it away, but I was nervous and I felt like it wouldn't be okay. Getting out of the car and we both start walking down this long path to the door. Feeling like I was walking down a long dark road to unknown light. Getting closer to the door, my heart starting pounding like it was a drummer beating faster and faster the closer we got. As we stepped into the front door, we were standing right in front of the school office. I needed positivity and gained that when we walked into the office and the first smile was from the school administrator. She really warmed my heart to the core, I needed that at that moment. I could tell that she knew my grandmother because of the way they were chatting. They made small talk about each other's family and how was their holiday. Their conversation gave me the chance to just look around. I wanted to see my surroundings and to see how different it was compared to my other schools.

This school was different from my last one. It had cleaner hallways and the classrooms rooms had doors. Another key takeaway was that this school was filled with different people of race. I have always been in school with only African American students. Even down to the teachers, so this was very new. I couldn't believe it. You can tell the kids knew I was new because as they came in the door to school they were waving and saying good morning to the administrator and were looking at me with the who are you look? I know that look all too well. I was more in awe of the fact that I was in school with people who didn't just look like me.

My thoughts ended when the wonderful receptionist smiled and told me how pretty I was and how cute my outfit was. I smiled a bit, as it was comforting to my ears. Wearing a purple sweatsuit with little shooting stars in bright colors. Thinking it had been a carebear sweatsuit. My hair had multiple ponytails with bows that matched my outfit and white tennis shoes. Can't believe my grandmother trusted me in white tennis shoes. She should know that we actually have recess, but then again, she hasn't done this in a while. Ensuring my grandmother, I would be fine making sure I got to my classroom. The teacher was expecting me and she was making sure I got to the bus after school. Now a city bus I was used to, but a school bus was new. I would catch it now and then when living with my aunt. Now I'm catching the bus every day. I guess the receptionist senses my nervousness and gave me a tender rub on my back. That touch was priceless. I've never felt that before, but it was what I needed at that moment. Her voice was so peaceful, it actually put me at ease. As my grandmother grabbed her purse, she looked at me with her brown strong eyes and told me that I would have a good day and she would see me when I got home. There was no hug, no kiss, no pat on the back, but she did at least say it would be fine and have a good day. The ladies said bye to each other and my grandmother went on with her day.

The receptionist helped me grab my little pink book bag, and we walked slowly down to my new class. This walk seemed like another prolonged event, as my nerves are not all over the place already. As we walked, I saw the pictures from the students on the walls and the receptionist talked to me as we continue to walk to my class. She told me funny jokes which gave me something to smile and giggle a little about right when we got to the door of my new classroom. As one student open the door, the receptionist held my hand as we walked into the classroom. I squeeze her hands because I was nervous. But my new teacher wasn't at all. All the kids were sitting, talking, and looking at me. I felt so out of place, I'm not used to being in a place so diverse.

The teacher came over to greet us and begin to talk to the receptionist, all I could think about was this is my fifth elementary school in five years and this is just the fourth grade. I am in a town that is small and lives in a house that has cows in front of it and drinking well water. After a few moments have passed, my thoughts were interrupted when the teacher spoke to me. Her voice was sweet and peaceful to me and she seems so nice. As her words were simple, they changed my entire life that day. All she said to me was welcome to F. T. Corry Elementary School and welcome to your new fourth-grade class. She introduces me to my new classmates, hugged me, told me how excited she was to have me in her class, and then showed me to my seat. I sat down, smiled, and looked around in amazement of being somewhere very different for once in my life. Tuesday, December 1, 1992, became my new everything.

"For which cause we faint not; but though our outward man perish, yet the inward man is renewed day by day."

– 2 Corinthians 4:16 KJV

Chapter Nine

Release

"Being free isn't just in the body, but the mind and soul."

Shatoria C

In 1995 I was in the middle of my sixth-grade year and there was too much going on at home, school, and in my head. So, my grandparents decided it was time for me to see a counselor. I didn't know what this would intel, but I had to go as it became a court order. I didn't have a choice by this time, many things started to change for me. The last three years have been tough because I had to adjust and understand the new location, making new friends, and trying to keep up with my grades. I wanted to fit in, but that wasn't going so well for me. I wanted to be free and I couldn't seem to find it or obtain it. There were many days I would come home from school in tears as I was trying to find my place with the other people. I was also being called names and picked on because my grandmother believes in us wearing dresses with ribbons and bows to school. The kids just talked about me and didn't care how I felt about it. Sure, they were kids, but they were cruel to the core.

As I'm sitting in the counselor's office, I looked around the small space t she had. She was sweet, but she learned quickly that I didn't want to answer questions. I'm nervous. I remember her asking me was I going back to our mother? Her eyes became very wide to my answer. I guess I was very blunt with her with a hard NO. I told her I didn't want to move again, so I stayed with my grandparents. I even threw in that she doesn't want me even if I went to live with her! With such base in my voice, the counselor ended up adjusting her seat. She asked me how did I feel? I remember telling her that I feel like she doesn't like me. I don't understand why my mother doesn't like me, but she didn't. My mother got herself together and still calls me names and likes to yell at me. My grandparents got to a point where they cut our mother off from talking to us. I felt like I was too much of a burden because I didn't understand why she didn't want me. She went and got married again, I honestly believe that she would not act right because she did this before. Could she stay clean long enough this time? I didn't want to get to her and then have to go back as this was a repeat pattern.

The counselor asked how do I allow my anger to come out? Did I want to tell her? I feel she knows and me tugging on my shirt sleeves isn't helping it. So, I should just say it and let it out. I explained to her about my cutting. My answer took her by surprise. Being that I'm 12, I explained in the best form that I could that cutting allows me to not feel. She asked me how long have I been cutting? With a lump in my throat, I said since I was 10. Her slim face that had a slight smile as she spoke with me became very grim in the eyes when I told her the starting age of cutting. I figured she has seen and heard it all, but I guess not. She wanted to know the story, and I started to explain to her my story and why I felt like I have.

It started in the fifth grade and it was a day that was like any other day. get up and go to school, but I have had battles that at my age, I shouldn't be fighting. I couldn't read or do math that well, and it was becoming noticeable. My mother had gotten married went to get her help and ended up getting married. The worst was I started my cycle at ten and I didn't know if this was normal or not. I learned a lot as a child that I shouldn't know at all. So, I just did what I would normally do to maybe help me feel a little better. Cry like a baby alone, write a letter saying that I was stupid and not beautiful, and then I would cut. This was never-ending cycling as I would do the same almost every day. It was way too much for my little mind. Honestly, I wanted that pain to end. The pain was like a burn that consumes my soul. I hated everything about me because it seemed like I wasn't good or worthy of enough to anyone. Don't know if it was my looks, the way I talked, the fact that I talked a lot to cover up my issues, my face, my build, or my hair. Just about everything that made me me seemed to be a negative in the eyes of others.

Speaking of that last thought, the counselor grabs my hand to embrace me. She cleared her throat and ask how I even started with the process. I readjusted myself in my seat and started explaining to her about going into the bathroom and seeing my grandfather shaving his face. He had a box of razors and he would say be careful as they were sharp and you can hurt yourself. How bad could it hurt? My grandfather gave a slight smile and answered with a simple "very bad if you not careful." I wanted to be free so bad that at this point I would do anything, so I felt like this could be it. After another day of dealing with being picked on, cutting was something I wanted to try to see what would I feel. Never used a razor before, but I have watched my grandfather for some time to understand how he shaved. Rumbling inside the bathroom three-drawer table and saw the small box of razors. Placing them on the counter and open the box to see them shining. My grandfather explaining to me how sharp they were played in my head, but I wanted to see for myself. Taking one of them out and looked down at my arm. I took the razor and slowly ran it up and down my arm and it stings a bit. The feeling that I had was a sting like getting the flu shot. I started to see blood and I felt like my breathing were quick but seeing the blood was a sign of release. This was my first time cutting, but it quickly became a nightly thing. My grandparents paid no mind to my arms and what I was doing, but I was feeling good for a moment. Just like using drugs, the feelings last for a moment.

The counselor didn't seem shocked or moved, but concerned. She asked me how I'm feeling at this point of my life with the cutting. I told her I felt free. Even if it is for a moment. Cutting was like my cries that no one could hear or see. It became part of my daily routine in my life. It also didn't help with sleep as I was still having sleepless nights. The counselor wanted to know what I was doing to sleep, and I explained that music was something I love. I would listen to the boombox at night and go back to sleep. She explained to me how my mother's drugs were the same as my drugs. Cutting was a drug, and it was controlling all parts of me. She wonders if we could replace it with something else. There was nothing to replace it with. I felt like the scars from the cutting were my battle wounds. For every time someone talked about me, I cut. For when my mother calls and tells me I'm a no-good child, I cut. It was no escaping it, so I did it because it gives me just a minute of peace and release from everything around me. No, it didn't last long, but long enough for me to just not feel or care. I wanted to be free so badly that it didn't matter, I just needed it.

People find freedom in different forms that are important to them. Good and bad, they figure it out. For me, cutting was my go-to thing as cutting gave me a little time of silence. I found this silence in our bathroom with my grandfather's razors. I figured the counselor thought something was wrong with me. I explained to her that watching myself do this was my way of screaming and not having to explain why I was screaming. But....it was only for a moment. I let it all out to her. She slowly closed her book and told me I had a lot on my plate. She even told me I have had a rough life, but that I need to remember some things. One thing for sure is that I am wanted. I am smart and I could do so much. She also explained that my grandparents are older, so they are still learning. They have spent many hours trying to understand, teach me and give me what I need because they are new to this. The counselor asked me a question that still haunts me now, but it didn't faze me then. She asked,

"If you take your own life, do you think anyone would truly miss you?"

I gave her an honest answer. No one! Looking down at her book and she gave me a slight smile. She wanted to send me home with homework and send my grandparents with tools to help with the process. Starting with writing positive things about me. The counselor felt like this was going to be a good start and to bring it to the next appointment. Writing positive things about myself wasn't easy and more so as I didn't believe in the positive words. I did it anyway but it wasn't working as my mother's words were counteractive to the positive that I was writing. In reality, my mother was my biggest bully. Couldn't catch a break from it and as time went on so did the cutting.

Cutting became the norm and was part of my life. As my grandparents never spoke to me about it, I believed they knew I was still doing it. They didn't ask, so I didn't bother telling them what was going on. I wished I wasn't feeling this way every day. The feeling like I had nothing to live for and just wanting to be free. Learning later as an adult is that freedom comes in many forms, including Christ. The counselor said it best that cutting is a drug that you have to stay high on to make it to the next step of the day. She also confirmed that it's also damaging to the body and the mind. Cutting was my primary drug in my life. I kept cutting until later in high school. Cutting went by the wayside as I found another primary drug. One thing about this new drug is that I didn't know the power and strength it carried, but what it did do is show me my true self and I didn't like what I was seeing.

"Stand fast therefore in liberty wherewith Christ hath made us free, and be not entangled again with the yoke of bondage."

– Galatians 5:1 KJV

Chapter Ten

The Many Encounters

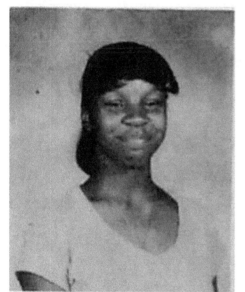 

"Loving me when others are not."

Shatoria C.

At the beginning age of 12, I noticed and saw many changes that were happening around me. It wasn't just within the moving to another grade, but also how I was dressing for school. My grandmother allowed me to wear what I wanted. She even took away the ribbons and bows from my hair and that made me feel better about myself, but just a little. The freedom of not wearing these items seems like I lost the weight I was carrying. However, the biggest change I noticed was my body. I notice my shape-changing and I was beginning to form from a girl to a young lady. I wasn't this little girl anymore with no chest to fill up, not even a sports bra. I was very small, my clothes felt different and I look different in them. I didn't know that was a big thing at that age, but it was as I wasn't the only one who took notice. Along with the changes physically, I changed socially as well. I formed genuine friendships with others. I tried out new things like being in the school band and JROTC. Even though I found out who I was, some parts didn't change. I still had things in school that were bothersome and so was my home life. Some kids still picked on me a little and some days were hard trying to adjust to growing up. I kept with my routine of going home and cutting and acting like everything was okay with me. People were talking about me and weren't about me cutting myself. It was my other drug, which became the round table talk.

Body changes became more of conversations for me. Boys would say how cute I was and with my low self-esteem, I went for it. I thought they liked ME. Not what I could offer, but for me. I soon found out this wasn't true at all. When I like, I liked hard, and this became a big problem for me as the feelings weren't the same. Physical relationships were the norm as I would like someone and they would express likeness as well. I would sleep with them as a sign of my likeness and problems started. This became a bad habit, and that grew into having relations with different people, different attachments, and more problems. I had no one at home talking about the birds and the bees to me and what it meant. Without actually having this conversation, I depended on the show and tell method. This is how I was taught things. Emotionally I was attached to anyone that gave me notice and it became a point of they give me notice long enough than I was giving them the physical part of me. This give and take relationship became the norm of my life. I've had sex before and was discarded later as if I didn't matter.

The depth of my emotional and physical endurance was becoming twisted together like a rope. I felt like this same rope was around my neck and every time I gave myself away from both physically and emotionally, it was getting tighter and tighter. There were moments in my life where I felt like I had died and even though I wasn't physically dead, I was emotionally dead. As the years flowed on, I begin to not care as having sex became an important thing. This was my way to express to the person I was dating or just having a fling with, how I felt without thinking that this wasn't the way to go about it. I had boyfriends and then there were the flings. The flings that I felt like I liked enough, but learned that they didn't like me enough to have more. I wasn't worthy of more according to the flings, but the boyfriends weren't as bad. However, I didn't know how to hold on to a relationship. I was young, looked for the wrong thing, and was trying to find my place with someone. What I desired from the boyfriends was causing issues. They didn't know what to give me because I didn't know what I needed.

Over time, there were stories of me going around. Not true, but it was easier to believe the lie, and I worked to live up to that same lie. The lies pushed more guys my way, and I worked to deal with them. Spending my time fighting battles that were created because of the things that were being said. Parts were true and much were false, but it was easier to play the part and deal with it. What my classmates and family didn't know was I hated life to the tenth power and my escape from it all was causing me more problems. I notice the more things were being said, the more I threw myself into sex. Sex was the biggest drug I had and the answer to everything. It made me feel whole and wanted, but that feeling lasted for a very brief time.

My smile was covering up things I had on my plate that people didn't see. They didn't see that I had absentee parents, abused as a child, molested for over a year, and cutting to release whatever I was feeling. Being hurt by the boys wasn't my true heartbreak. My heartbreak was when I lost a great friend the summer before high school, and my life became upside down. After his death, I couldn't contain my emotions and my behavior actions had gotten out of control. My sexual partners had already started with the two males before, but now, they all started to become a blur.

My feelings were wrapped up in boys. I don't know how I kept up with grades, but from my friend's death till well into adulthood my life twisted with sex like it was a spiderweb. I craved and needed it and the whole time I was damaging my soul, my thoughts, my feelings, and my emotions. Every time I laid down with someone it was another step towards the death of my soul. Sharing my body with boys who cared less about my mind, dreams, or goals became normal and was also slowly killing me inside.

After the death of my friend, I had to deal with death again with my uncle. I kept smiling and going with life and my behavior with boys just got worse. I was stacking up my number of people I slept with and lost so much respect for myself. I didn't know what respect was anymore, and I wasn't smart when it came to my emotional side. I allowed sex to run my life and my feelings for everything. With no proper guidance and tools for my growth, I was going nowhere fast. Reality became being left by the boys I thought liked me, talked about by those that spoke of friendship, and is one of my worst enemies. Being physical and emotionally abandoned was normal and surprise to those who stayed to be a part of my life in any form. I question people if they stayed because this wasn't normal for me. What was it about me for them to want to be with me and many would say that I was really beautiful and had a lot going for myself. With this knowledge, it did nothing for me. I didn't want a good guy. I didn't see good guys. I like the rough, around the edge dude who had a controlling trait about him. This was what I was used to seeing, and I thought this was the right way. Man, was I all the way wrong. I have lost many relationships and many good men behind this thought process. Those thoughts cost me a lot of good relationships and even friendships along with way.

Being an adult with the mindset of a child didn't help me. From being that young teenager to an adult, I still couldn't get it right. I looked and looked for the love and attention and the way I felt like it was going to be found was between my legs. I used men for a good time because I needed a fix. Many called it their hoe days, but mine went on for years. I got bored quickly and needed something new. As I allowed myself to be used and use people, the number count of people in my life grew. I lost count, but I know the number wasn't small. Many have said I was crazy for even thinking of all the men I have had in my life, but each one played a part in my growth.

No matter how I look at it, sex was a powerful drug that played a big part in how I operated in my life. I got to the point where I would have sex and move on because I would not allow another person to tell me they didn't want me. This was a merry-go-round that wouldn't end. I wanted to be wanted for not what I could give physically, but mentally and spiritually. I was broken in all of those areas. It took me years to know my worth and what I was worthy of. It took me crying and saying what I have done to myself. I am not ashamed of what happened in my life. I'm not proud either Yes, I had many partners, taking my life and placing it in other people's hands, and losing control of myself. I have no fear of my past and what it can bring. I don't worry about what others think of my sexual activities even as I write this. I learned as an adult how to control my life's narrative and I some point I finally got it.

It has freed me from the feeling of wondering what others think and feel of me. I don't have to prove anything about who I am by using parts of me. The parts of me are beautiful and should be embraced as such. The men I slept with no longer belong to me. So, talk about me if you desire. I'm not moved. Call me names because of what I did. It is okay, as it doesn't bother me anymore. The reason I am so happy and in a better place with it all is because it has released me from those men and I no longer hold those numbers.

"Stand fast therefore in the liberty wherewith Christ hath made us free, and be not entangled again with the yoke of bondage"

-Galatians 5:1 KJV

Chapter Eleven

Thirty Day Shift

"You are fearless."

Shatoria C

The heart wants what the heart wants. There were so many things I wanted and desired, but deep down in my heart, I didn't know how to filter what was good and what wasn't for me. I had a void to be filled, and I was seeking it without knowing what it was I was seeking. I attached myself to many men over a short period. There was the physical side and a very tiny portion was romantical. Having a boyfriend wasn't the issue, but staying focus and keeping the relationship was a fight that was partially on me. The relationship could be good, but when sex came to play, I would soon get bored with them, and then my interest was lost after a while. The characteristics that I was seeking in these so-called men were crazy. Their traits weren't the best, but I figured why not? I think I was so numb to being hurt that I looked pass things and rolled with the flow. My thoughts for men were mostly sexual. I fell in love with the sex and not the person. The types of men I encounter in my life were all very different from each other. They were so different in every way possible.

My soul was twisted like a boat knot and it was getting worse. After high school, I thought I could handle being out as a college student and working full time. I couldn't have been more wrong. There were people in my life and some didn't showcase positive relationships of any kind. I went along with it because they gave me a good time. The men in my life were all different as there was one living the drug life, another man who didn't work and weren't going to, and a man from Haiti who was fun to be around, but just for that. He was my most adventurous one, and we both understood each other. I like him more but didn't want a relationship for many reasons. They all had one thing in common and that was they carried energies and I feed off of them. Their energy was a daily meal for my soul and I was getting fat off of it.

My thirst for short-term attention grew, and I needed something different all the time. Being in the young adult stage of life, my insecurities were showing their ugly head. I felt no one wanted to deal with any of my flaws, and I didn't either. I stopped caring about if I was a good girl because all I wanted was to be wanted. The reason remained a mystery for a while. I became so content with where I was, but clearly, that was in my head, as my heart and feelings didn't match my thoughts. I was playing a very dangerous game. With my life and my body for sure. The outer part of me was dressed up differently than my spirit. By being in school and working full time, I believe in working hard to do better. There was a lot below that at first glance couldn't be seen, but it slowly became a noticeable annoyance among some, but mostly myself.

I have been told so many things about myself and didn't believe the worthiness of myself. Now I believed the negative, as it seemed to be easier to live up to. My grandparents spent eight years trying to keep me from the life I was creating, but I wasn't listening. They wanted me to stand out, but not the way I was going about it. For 18 months, I stayed in the club, drinking, meeting guys, and as people say, living my best life. I became bored quickly, which pushes me into the arms of men who meant me no good. Now, even though they meant no good, I knew what I was doing and I became selfish and reckless with my life. With no kids or husband to live or do right by I did what I felt. I desired to live a good life, but I honestly didn't know-how.

As I was being reckless, some were in silence with their prayers and always showing me love no matter how my life was looking. I wanted to change, but there wasn't a reason to change according to my view. I lost a lot of me with giving myself away to too many men, but people period. Not sexual, but just always being there and trying to save people from themselves. I couldn't find or get fulfillment for anything or anyone, and with that, I remained empty. Spiritually, physically, and emotionally empty. I worked to see that people had good intentions, and I don't know why when my taste in men was bad. Placing trust in many and no matter what; they hurt me in the end. Over time, nothing changed, and I became bitter with life. One thing I didn't lose was my thought process about the word. My grandparents are to thank for that as they kept us in church. I didn't know the Bible front and back, but I knew deep down that my lifestyle wasn't right. With time, things stayed the same, and I went on about life until I finally met someone.

This guy was very different and had a way with words. We will call him "Dee" for the moment. Dee's body build was skinny and wasn't any bigger than my pinky. His skin tone was such a beautiful caramel brown, and it was accompanied by the cutest baby face you could see. He had a cheerful voice that carried a sexy tone with it. I met him when I was out at a family event and minding my business. Out of nowhere, I hear this hello as I'm grabbing food. He found his way over to me and he had me at hello. He flirted and after a brief conversation, I flirted back. We ended up talking a little longer and exchanged numbers. We dated only for six months, but a lot took place at that time. As the relationship started on a high note, it stayed that way as I felt for a good period. We had fun in the relationship. We met each other's families, spent weekends with each other. We had dates that were simple because he tried to be romantic, but he was not the smartest in that. Having sex didn't get introduced until the third month of dating. In a short time, we felt like we were the one for each other. Our love was strong and I couldn't have been happier, but then Dee hit me with something at the beginning of our six months of dating.

We were on a date bowling and having a great time. When it was time for us to leave, we started walking to the car. I can't remember all of the conversations, but he asked about me living with him. Don't know what it was, but I have never been comfortable living with a dude. Maybe it was how I said it or what I said, but he didn't like it. I remember him grabbing my neck and pinning me to the car. Our eyes locked and what I saw wasn't the Dee I had been dating. All I knew was it caught me off guard and he quickly came back to himself. He kept saying he was sorry, and he didn't know what had gotten into him. I didn't know what had happened but all I did was hug him. I don't know why, but I did. We said we loved each other, and he opens the door to the car for me to get in. We acted as if nothing had happened and even though we acted like it, I remember sitting down wondering what just happened? But for the life of me, couldn't answer that question. The drive back to my mother's home was silent and not much was being spoken. Arriving home, I guess Dee felt he needed to break the ice. He said he loved me and asked about taking our relationship to the next level. I think I blacked out because he asked me to marry him.

Wait a minute... did he just ask me that question? He was on his knees and saying he was sorry about earlier and asking me to be his wife? I couldn't hear anything, but he took me out of my daze when he tapped me and said my name. I looked into his eyes and he said again how sorry he was. All I remember coming out of my mouth was yes. I don't know why I said it, but I did. He was happy, but he was shaking. Not like a nervous shake, but he was shaking. I brushed it off and hugged him. With no ring, we at least had one thing, and that was so much love for each other. I was really on cloud nine and at the young age of 19, I felt like I was winning. That was on the surface, but deep down, I was scared and I didn't know how to get out of it. I kept it to myself that I was scared. Dee had to tell people, so I had to tell my mother. I played the part for sure because I didn't want to give up what was going on or how I felt.

As the sixth month carried on, you couldn't tell me anything as I was planning a wedding. Hoping I could be a good wife as I know being a girlfriend hasn't been easy for me before. I couldn't believe I had someone who wanted to go to this level with me as I have always questioned myself and usually my relationships were based on sex. Could this be real? Being in love this quickly? I was blinded by what I felt was love, and slowly my blinders started to clear up. I think they cleared up that night when he put his hands around my neck. As I took a little more time to learn about him, I compared it to what we used to be and how we started. He seemed to have issues that I later learned I just missed the signs of them. I missed a lot honestly, and I was a fool in love or what I thought was love. I started paying attention to his changes as they bloomed like a rose in a garden.

As the days moved forward, I started to plan our life together. I saw he had a lot of demons and we started to not get along. It started with our conversations. My once baby face-looking love had lost so much weight in all aspects. He looked different, but my love and care remained the same. I truly cared for him in every way, and I felt I could help. I didn't want to give up on him, and he didn't want me to give up either. I thought he was getting better; he was getting worse. I acted as if I didn't see what was going on, but I knew better. I felt like we were a great match, but there were thoughts about that night when he choked me. I wanted his love, and for him to fill the void that I carried, I thought he was doing just that. I soon noticed other things that were filing whatever he felt he was missing from me.

It would have been great if it was another girl he was sleeping with or maybe he felt I wasn't performing. His void wasn't another female, it was needles in his arm. He was fighting things I couldn't save him from. Trust me, I tried. With me taking on his issues, my issues became hard to bear. I learned in a brief time that no matter what we had in common, I couldn't do anything for him.

Thinking this was a phase and he will change. Having hope but our relationship got worse as his drug use grew. While the use of drugs grew, so did the vulgar and out-of-line comments he would make towards me. There were days I didn't know who I was engaged to. I transformed into what he wanted and how he wanted things to be. He was planning out how everything was going to go when we got married. He picked a June 2002 date and started to plan. My soul was so attached to his to where I couldn't tell who I was on a good day. My daily goals became his, and I was being reminded by others around me I couldn't save him. I know now I was foolish, but couldn't see it before. Not knowing how broken I was until the day he put his hands on me to where I had to work to hide the mark. Appalled at the fact that he was bold enough to do it, I still told him I loved him. Acting as nothing has happened, I kept with the planning of our wedding. Staying with him through it all along, giving myself to him freely. More than just broken; I was a damaged soul.

I was numb to some things that he would say and do. Even allowing him to tell me who I was for him and to him. Becoming a slave to his demands and his way of life. It didn't stop him from putting his hands on me and seeing me as a sex slave. He would remind me that no one wanted me but him and that I would never go anywhere. I belonged to him and him alone. I believed him and all his words. Dee was powerful with words, and I was weak-minded. So, it made his words strong to a weak-hearted person. He controlled our relationship with sex and his weird demands. No control over my life anymore I felt weak at the thought of being a wife to a person who I was becoming scared of. I was working at Burger King and wasn't making a lot of money, but I made sure Dee was good at all times. My feelings were that this was true genuine love, but this wasn't it. I don't know what you called this because it was more than lust.

Draining was the feeling I felt for the last month we were together. Those thirty days felt like a year with him. I remember talking to my grandmother and she notices things I didn't know she was paying attention to. She recommended I let him go before she will have to bury her first granddaughter at the young age of 19. Her words were short but powerful with the truth. She said to me that my soul was tied to him and I was becoming him. I didn't know my family saw my life this way just like not knowing that I wasn't being me anymore. Feeling like a disappointment to my grandparents and all that they worked for to get me to where I am. The biggest question in my life was where am I going? I wasn't a lazy person, I was working full time at my job even though it was a burger joint. I had a high school education and some college. I needed to make moves and Dee was holding me back. What Dee didn't know was that I was working to make moves, and I held it up because I was seeing where we were going.

For five months, I went from being on happy drugs in a relationship to getting into our sixth month where I became beaten and broken from a person, I felt I loved and thought loved me. I destroyed myself by holding on to a man who wanted to be in control of it all, and I couldn't help but try to be all that he needed and wanted. The amount of time we dated destroyed my soul in a way that I couldn't see what was next. I worked to keep up the smile, but my soul looked like it was part of a fire and you couldn't recognize me in flesh or spirit. No matter how much my soul longed for Dee, I couldn't take another beating or a wild night of sex. But that didn't matter, because I still longed for him. What I knew was I was settling as I have always done with every guy I have come in contact with. I prayed for a quick change as I was unhappy. That prayer seemed to be answered quickly as I don't know what happen to this day with Dee. He disappeared and we went from calls sometimes to the calls just stopping.

Within 30 days, I got engaged, got my ass beat, and he disappeared into the wind. So, since he wasn't in my life anymore, I found others. It became a game for me, and I had my way with whoever I felt. We all had an understanding that I didn't want anything but that. Wanting nothing but sex was a lie that I kept telling myself. I wanted to be treated right, but since that wasn't working out so well, I gave them what they wanted. After a while, I noticed I became embodied with people's spirits once more and couldn't find any way to release myself from it. Feeling like the men were demons sucking my soul from my body, and I allowed it every time with each of them. I was destroying myself with thoughts of the care for my well-being or my safety, to be honest. Sometimes I was careful and times I wasn't. I just did what I wanted to do and where. I had no respect for myself, or anyone else. My outer self looked fine with the smile and always laughing. My spirit was tired, hurting, and slowly dying. I honestly didn't know what to do or how to give it life again, but what I couldn't believe was how I was living. My only way to getting my life together was to escape. Don't know where I was going to go with no money and no real job. I didn't want to go back to Greensboro to live with my grandparents, even though they wouldn't say no. My escape this time needed to benefit me and far from here. I had an idea and I was a little bit scared of the idea.

In 18 months, 545 days, about 13,080 hours, I was able to tie myself up spiritually in a way that I lost all control of my life. Within those 18 months, five months were awesome while I was wearing blinders, but in that sixth month, I almost lost my life trying to be, do, and keep something that wasn't for me. My escape was near and I needed this. I felt like the kid who had the stick with a little cloth tied to it and was leaving by walking away singing. Destroying myself was easy, but now it's time to rebuild. This process was going to take me out of my comfort zone and force me to work on myself. What Dee didn't know is that I was already working on plans, but I put those plans to the side when I met Dee. Now it was time to reactivity those plans again and follow what I need to do. To do that, I need to start back from the beginning, which started as a beautiful Tuesday morning.

"For the mountains shall depart, and the hills be removed; but my kindness shall not depart from thee, neither shall the covenant of my peace be removed, saith the Lord that hath mercy on thee."

Isaiah 54:10 KJV

Chapter Twelve

The Great Escape

"Run into your destiny as it waits for you."

Shatoria C

I attended a community college in Decatur, Georgia, right after high school. My goal was to go to a community college and then transfer to my dream school, which was Duke University in North Carolina. I wanted to be a teacher and be the first to graduate from college. I had a load of dreams and I started it by attending Georgia Perimeter College and working full time at Taco Bell. My goal was to get money to help me attend Duke, it wasn't cheap. I was blessed to have had received a small scholarship to at least attend the community college.

Just like that little girl with the missing tooth enjoyed school then, I enjoyed being in college. It was a sense of freedom, meeting new people, and they didn't know much about me. This was a great start to something new. School started that August and I enjoyed all of it. I had classes every day, and I was working. I didn't get much sleep, because of the schedule I had. Monday and Wednesday were three classes a day, Tuesday and Thursday I had two classes, and Fridays were one class. My day was the same. I would get up at five in the morning to catch the bus, then the train, to catch another bus. It took me about two hours or more to get from home to school and the same going back. Once school was over and I got home, I prepped for work. Working at Taco Bell full time was a lot because I would get to work about four or five in the afternoon and work till closing. That left me with about 3 hours in a day to study and with 5 classes I had a lot on my plate. I felt like I could handle it all while I had on my cape with the big letter S.

Tuesday morning, September 11, 2001, I just finished one of my

English college classes for the day. Between classes, I made my way to the common area with a group of friends, we had one more class to go to. The common area was a large space that looked like a café with a concession stand at a game. We grabbed a table to chat, I grabbed some fries to snack on. Our table was right in line with the big television that was like an enormous square box that was sitting on the floor. As we are talking and watching the television, I thought it was a movie we were watching. I watched this plane go into a building and I watch the building fall. Caught off guard by what I was seeing and didn't know how to react. We all went on back to eating and soon went to the next class. No one really could or would speak on the issue as no one knew what was going on. At the end of class, I left to go home. My way of transportation was the bus and the train and today I caught it just in time as they shut down transportations across the state of Georgia. My young-minded self was in disbelief that they dared to shut things down because this was my only mode of transportation and whatever that was going on wasn't in Georgia.

As this day went on, I found a way to work and went on about my day. People were talking, but nothing really in stone. I listened, and I worked but didn't take anything in. After a couple of days, I started to watch the news. It gave me some insight into what was really going on and the story unfolded. That is not what got my mind spinning and deep in thoughts. I spent time in JROTC and I know that military uniform. My grandparents wanted me to go into the military once I graduated from high school, but I thought I was grown and wanted to make a point. I thought about going but that was short-lived. I looked around at what I was doing with my life at that moment, and I didn't like what I was seeing. It wasn't enough to change anything, even though changes needed to happen. All I needed to do is to go to a recruiter, but with school and work, I couldn't find the time.

With the world trying to put itself back together from 911, I had to go back to work like nothing had happened or changed. I still pondered about leaving but didn't know how bad I needed to leave. It wasn't a top priority. Work gave me some pride, but it was helping me with bills and my going out. I felt a place at work as I was the oldest worker outside of the managers. A place with set hours for the lobby and drive-through. Our lobby closed at nine in the evening and the drive-thru at ten. Another life-changing moment awaited me, and it wasn't pretty. On Thursday, October 25, 2001, I was working the night shift. We had a new manager, and he was young. I was the front cashier for the day and also since I was the oldest, the manager felt it was my duty to make sure everyone was ready to go that was in the back. Noticing the time, it was almost ten, and the lobby was still open. I informed the manager that we needed to close the lobby so we can clean and get everyone out and home in a timely matter because we all had school the next day. And by the way, the lobby doors were supposed to have locked at nine. He ensured me he was going to go over and get it done. What happens next triggered my anxiety to another level.

I didn't see anything coming. I wished I had because I was

cleaning the counters by the registers, and all I saw were two young boys rushing into the restaurant banishing guns. The manager ran like a track runner and jumped over the trashcans and out the back door. He left four young kids, including me, in this restaurant alone and scared. It was a little over a week before my 19th birthday and all I see are two young men with guns to my head and asking me for the combination of the store safe. As they were trying to open it, there was a young lady who had a phone. We needed help so, I mouthed to her to text someone for help. You could see the fear through her eyes. I was scared out of my mind but needed to give them all I had. She understood what I said, and she did it. The guys worked hard to get that safe open and just couldn't get it done. They got upset, and they left at the same time they heard the police sound.

What I couldn't get out of my head was the vision that was my life and a gun right in front of my face. This is how my life was going to end? I had so many questions as I wonder why in the world did the manager leaves us there? Not returning to work for a while, I still went to school and was shaken up still. I needed some time to adjust to what had happened. There are things you don't forget and one thing I didn't forget was that the young men had their faces covered, but you can see their eyes. Those eyes I wouldn't ever forget. Unfortunately, a week later, those same young men went into another Taco Bell that wasn't too far from the one I worked and took lives. They took four lives that Friday night. It was the day before my 19th birthday and I remember the news showing their mug shot. I saw the eyes, and I knew it was them. This time they were bold and killed them execution-style. They killed a sixteen- year old and the manager who was in their early twenty's. I count my blessing that I have been able to see another birthday after all of this. With 911 and this new event staring me in my face, I didn't know if I would see the next day. My grandparents became concerned more and more. The gun in my face was the nail in the coffin. They told me their concerns about being back in the city and not leaving to go into the military. I was rethinking it and finally went to see the recruiter. I am very grateful I made this decision and my family seems to be excited too.

I left for the military on October 1, 2002, which was seven months after the longest 30-day shift of my life. These were new beginnings for me as I needed this break. This was supposed to be a clean break to start over with people who don't know me or my struggles. I had no actual goals going into the military. What I knew for sure is that this was my great escape from this life. My emotions were all over the place because now I'm really on my own. Away from my family as I was in another entire state all by myself. I was alone and not physically, but emotionally and mentally. God got me through my dark days as I learned a lot about myself and my demons during this process. This was a process within itself. I figured my demons would stay back in Georgia where I felt like I left everything. I remember being on that plane flying out of Georgia and looking over at the clouds. I thought I was leaving all my issues behind, but on February 12, 2003, those issues, hurt, and pain grew wings and they all found me good old Texas.

"Therefore if any man be in Christ, he is a new creature: old things are passed away; behold, all things are become new."

2 Corinthians 5:17 KJV

Chapter Thirteen

Stepping from Death to Healing

"Walk into your destiny."

Shatoria C

Being on my own for about four months was new, fun, and a vast of learning experiences. I had it in my head that I had every day to live out my life and determined to be different. Showing I was capable to handle myself and things around me. Something I have never questioned was that I had my beautiful grandparents who raised me and loved me with their whole heart. I wanted to make sure they were proud of me. Knowing they weren't happy with me not going into the military right after high school, but I have finally done it and they were excited about this new move.

Talking to my grandparents almost every day to tell them how life was going and my new adventures in Wichita Falls, Texas, within a month of being in the area, I gave my time at the Boys and Girls club. I loved this, I was working with young kids and teaching them. This was the kid's outlet, and we were doing simple things like crafting and sports. The best part was just spending time with them and watching them being kids. I love telling my grandparents what was going on and how life was. My grandmother and I did most of the talking, and my grandfather would just say a couple of very short words.

My grandfather wasn't a talker or a caller. I would have to call him to chat with him. He loved fishing and hunting. So usually during hunting season, he wasn't home, but he was finally home one cold day in February 2003. I was in my room studying and when my phone ring I show my grandmother's number. I surely thought it was my grandmother and to my surprise, it was my grandfather. He was calling just to see how I was. I told him about my day and what

I was doing. He asked about the kids at the Boys and Girls Club and how studying for work was going. We talked for a pretty good minute and I enjoyed all of it. I didn't feel weird at first until he said, I love you, to me. It was weird because this isn't something that is spoken in our family. I love you as a foreign sentence when it came from family. No matter how weird it was, I said it back, but I meant it because I loved my grandfather. He stepped in to raise me when I had no parents. This man had no children that were his by birth, but you would not tell him that. So, when he said I love you, I knew he really meant it and I took it in. We got off the phone and what I didn't know was that this would be my last time hearing his voice.

Wednesday, February 12, 2003, I came home from work and looked at my house phone to see that my grandmother and my mother had called. Telling myself that I would call them back as I needed to get down to the Boys and Girls Club to work. I went on about my evening at work and doing what I love to do. My drive home was about 15 minutes and halfway through the drive my cell phone rings. It was my grandmother and with my jolly self I answered the phone with:

"Sorry I was going to call you tomorrow, but had to work at the club."

Her voice came through the phone somber, and she asked me to pull over. I didn't like the sound of her voice, but I did what she asked. I told her I stopped and asked what was going on. She broke the news that my grandfather had surgery and was coming home

109

today. I had a slight smile on my face, but she broke it by telling me that instead of him coming home to her, he went home to be with the Lord. Confused, I didn't know he was that sick to need surgery. I felt like I lost everything in a blink of an eye. He was gone and wasn't coming back.

My grandparents didn't want to tell me about my grandfather being sick. I didn't know how sick or what type of sickness. He was under the weather when I graduated basic training, hence the reason they didn't make it to the ceremony. But sick enough for surgery and not to come home. It broke my heart. I lost my dad, my father, my grandfather on that cold day. He died in a hospital room alone. This man was the love of my life. He wasn't happy about me leaving home to go back to Atlanta right after high school. He rather that I stayed in Greensboro and worked until I left to go do something. His concerns were genuine. I had a lot of questions and a lot of why's, but this wasn't the time to ask. I gave my grandmother love and told her I needed a moment. Hanging up the phone, all I could do was scream and hit the steering wheel in so much pain. I did not understand and I had questioned God in many ways with why this happened. Knowing deep down that I would not get answers, and I just needed to take the evening to process all that had happened.

After informing my supervisor and making plans, I was on a plane back to Atlanta. When I saw my grandmother, I gave her the biggest hug. I actually slept in the bed with her that night. She kept a smile on her face no matter how she was feeling. That Saturday morning, I arranged my uniform so I could wear it for my grandfather. My grandmother told me how sharp he was going to be. She asked my cousin and me to stand at his casket. I agreed, but later wish I didn't. Walking into the church I grew up in with my grandparents and on my grandmothers' arm, I felt so much hurt. I saw my grandfather and I wished that he would wake up. Walking over to the smoke gray casket, and standing at the head of his casket, I worked hard to look strong. As everyone was walking in, I couldn't give off a smile and I got sick standing there. I held it together. I glance down to look at his face. He looked so peaceful. His suit matched his casket, and he had on this yellow tie. Because it was Valentine's Day weekend, there were so many red or pink and yellow carnations. I loved it, it was who he was. He was simple, and that was the man I remember. I felt my heart crash when they closed the casket and I heard that snap sound. I knew then I wouldn't see him anymore. My life changed, but I really don't know if it changed for the worse or the better. As you continue to read, you can make that judgment for yourself.

My grandmother wrote his obituary, and it read that he had a wife and two daughters. I asked my grandmother about it and she showed me the paperwork from the court. On this day I learned that my grandparents loved me enough to adopt me. That type of love melted my heart. He wanted me to know that he loved me whole heartily. Even though we were not blood-related the bond between us couldn't be broken. I wanted to make him so proud, but not just him, my grandmother, and my mother as well. My grandfather was my superhero, but I couldn't handle his death, and my return to Texas proved that with my behavior.

Getting back to Texas was like a light switch. I didn't know how to control my outrage, my mouth, my thoughts, and any of my movements. My lust for men climbed from the grave and soon trouble followed. Young, in pain, angry, and I miss my grandfather. I was hurting and desperate for things I couldn't control or have. As I started my journey in the middle of 2003, I learn some hard things about myself and that is I didn't handle certain things well. It took me a while to admit it and to understand that I needed help.

By the end of 2003, I lost full control over my thought process and behavior. I needed to get myself together; sooner than later and more positively. What I grasped in my life is that my grandfather's death allowed some issues to slap me right in my face. I felt like someone put a mirror directly in front of me and I saw myself facing myself and it wasn't pretty. I saw the little girl who was beaten, sexualize, abandon and lost. She stared at me and I stared back. All my issues were all bundled in that little person. I understood that inside of me was that little girl, and even though I was an adult, that little girl was still inside of me. It is time for a change and I need it fast because I am spiraling out of control and if I don't get this together, I'm heading down some unthinkable roads. I finally decided to do what I needed to do, and that was going to church and learning for myself. It was a positive change Because of the change, I became active again in the community and started to learn things about me and my walk with Christ. Stepping into church became my right place for my healing. This was my hospital, my peace, and a joy. The change was good, and doing so started my new journey in my life. I lived life and enjoyed it.

What I didn't know was that my grandfather's death was going to be the stepping stone to my healing. By going to church, learning my faith, and allowing God to use me for whatever reason became the rightest thing of my life. So much had happened in my life that I had to deal with each hurt bit by bit, but I was going to get through it. As I entered 2004 and 2005, things changed. I grew, met new people, and really flourish in both those years I started liturgical dancing for church, singing, and growing spiritually. I even got my first apartment all on my own. I believed that there was more to my life. For once in my life, I decided to have faith that there were good people and men out there. Between 2005-2009 I felt like I finally found a good one. But I wasn't ready for him, and he wasn't ready for me. I was still going through my healing process. This was an actual relationship that I wanted and I had to treat it differently. To get a different outcome, you have to do something different. So, I did.

NathaniE J. Perkins

(3 October 1933 – 12 February 2003)

"And the people, when they knew it, followed him: and he received them, and spake unto them of the kingdom of God, and healed them that had need of healing"

Luke 9:11 KJV

Chapter Fourteen

Soul Tied to the Soul

"Latch yourself to greatness."

Shatoria C.

As I was sitting in church, this lady was speaking about spirits that are like leeches. How they suck the life out of you and you become what they are. She was explaining how many people can be all over the place as they are attached to so many spirits. This day I felt she was talking about me. I had missed some church and the night before because I was laying up with a dude. By this time, I was working on me and my faith and I was growing, but some days I hit the ground hard. The woman kept speaking, and she talked about collecting spirits as our own. Every time we sleep with someone, we are collecting their spirit and whoever they slept with. I understood her fully as I started thinking over all those I have given my spirit to, and vice versa. All those years of relationships and why I was acting the way I was, was me taking on those spirits called soul ties.

I allowed my soul ties to have power over everything of and about me. I gave them power, and they used it to their full advantage. The power they held helped control my feelings and kept me in a space of loneliness and hurt. I'm sitting in this seat and listening to what the woman is saying about collecting spirits, and all I could think about is every man I allowed to enter me. The sadness that came over me consumed me because I didn't know what was my future with relationships with men. I allowed this spirit to engulf me and take over my life. I inhaled the smell and touch that it brought, completely avoiding the fact that it gave me pain and kept me in tears. I do understand that those spirits carried a beautiful and erotic smell. That smell was strong and had a very strong arm in maneuvering you into its presence. That is the type of spirit that I needed to get away from and one of the hardest spirits to let go of.

During my time of learning, growing, and trying to cleanse myself from these souls, I finally met a guy. I liked him. I wanted a relationship with him, but I didn't know if this would be different. There were a lot of requests that I needed to make and my concerns were if he would agree or disagree. At the age of 22 everyone, I have been with wasn't good for me and they weren't healthy either. I honestly didn't know if he would like me as I liked him. I knew little of him, but it was something about him that screamed different. I was just scared that I was blinded, and I didn't want to risk being wrong for the millionth time. So, I stepped out on faith, to see if I could try this differently. I was very opposite of social standards. When I spoke to him and we finally chatted, I told him I didn't want to kiss or have sex. I wanted to get to know him. I didn't tell him why, and he never asked. I was shocked at his response. I had enough spirits that I had to deal with and I didn't want to deal with more.

He took a chance with me and my "rules" as I say. He respected me and my space that I needed. As we later spoke about it, he wanted to respect what I wanted. Our courtship wasn't easy because we both had our own issues and that we were dealing with. I didn't want to add more issues to what was at hand. Purposely waited a year for anything intimate with him and I won't lie, I was surprised that he stayed. Not saying this process was easy, but faith was the key to this relationship. I couldn't believe I had a dude that didn't judge me for what my issues were and what I was trying to do to better myself. Even with my soul ties, we dated for five years off and on before marriage. He married me and my soul ties in 2010 and loved me. I couldn't believe I had a whole husband and a family, but I was still trapped. I honestly thought being married would free me from all the issues that I carried. What marriage did for me was allowed me to suppress them and stayed busy caring for others. It was damaging my soul by not releasing them. To add to the issues, I had to be honest with myself. I wasn't over the fact that I still had abandonment issues from my parents, my grandfather's passing, and all the men in my life. I knew I needed help, and I needed it fast.

I heard a woman speak about soul ties, and how they can affect your life. In early 2013, I attended this empowering encounter for women. Sitting in a local church in Tulsa, Oklahoma, during their annual encounter event. This allowed me to share this time with women who all felt like I did and felt like they were at their end. It felt great to speak and not be judged. Emotions, drugs, sex, and pain are strong when you are dependent on them. I depended on it like I needed water and food. I used the fact that I was having sex as a position and tool to get what I wanted. But I wasn't free at all. I felt trapped, like being in a coffin; dark and alone. Being part of this encounter was powerful. I could feel it when I walked through the doors. Feeling the weight of my load on me but being here allowed me to finally work to free myself of it. Learning to say it out loud was a freeing experience. I was used to writing out my issues, but to speak it was different. Freedom and forgiveness are what I needed and not just from sex, but life and the things attached to it.

The conference had hundreds of women attending the conference, and I had the chance to meet women who were feeling like I was feeling and dealing with what I was dealing with in my life. They placed us in groups that were about seven women. This allowed me to be one on one with others and hundreds of others who didn't know my business. This conference was allowing me to be the free person I wanted and needed to be. I didn't know what to expect and didn't know how this would feel, I was scared to be that free. People's thoughts of me were more important that I forgot I was stronger than my actions. My first concern was if people were going to accept me for my flaws or not, and honestly, their opinions shouldn't have even been a factor for me.

Being at this conference was the start of my new beginnings. People who don't know me or my spirit didn't judge me, and it was the greatest feeling because it allowed me to tell my story. They were giving us tasks and one task I felt I wasn't ready for. This task required me to be very honest about myself. If I didn't care about people's feelings of me, then I needed to take this step to be a better me for my family and myself. As it got closer to the next step, God reminded me He's not lukewarm and I needed to pick aside. As they instructed us to take a piece of paper, I had to cheer myself on. Could I do this and be this honest?

"Please write down every name of anyone that you have had any type of relations with. Also, write down anything that you are attached to."

I felt so overwhelmed and it was a lot for me to take in. Allowing

God to comfort me at this moment as I needed so much peace. Getting back to writing, I truly didn't remember all their names, and that part got to me. Pushing out a prayer so I can be comfortable and remember what I need to remember. After some time in prayer and allowing God to take the lead, I started to remember their scents, their words, their touch, and all the insignificant details, but names weren't coming to me unless I knew them personally. Feeling ashamed again, I didn't want to write or be part of this. In my head, I told myself I was a whore, slut, dirty, and a jezebel and that is how people saw me.

I got exasperated and anxious quickly. I looked around, and some were writing and some were not. My spirit became heavy again, so prayed silently one more time. I had to listen AND hear God. This time this prayer was different. I felt His peace cover me like a soft bed comforter. I write and as I wrote I could feel the spirits and I couldn't believe it. I wrote every name, and I didn't miss one. The names covered four pages and yes; I said four. I was in a daze as I wrote them all down. It was like I was blacked out for that moment. God allowed me to remember every spirit that has ever touched me in any way possible. As I wrote I shook, and that was because I felt like my spirit was fighting what I needed to do. I wrote every name, including my husband. Why did I add him since he is my husband? Because I was tied to the wrong part of his spirit. Yes, I may have waited a year into our relationship to have relations, but I did and he became a soul tied as well. I needed to be free of all wrong spirits and things that were holding me back.

Once we finished writing, I looked down and noticed I wrote without blinking an eye. I felt so different, and I was still shaking with fear. Starting to remember how each one of those names made me feel. Accepting the fact that I had every feeling that could come over me. The power I had right then was filled with anger, fire, pain, and hate. But when I wrote all of that down, I could feel the pain being released. It was almost like getting a deep tissue body massage. If you have ever had one of those, then you understand the feeling. My spirit was so heavy, but I felt something was different. I felt like something was moving out of me. It was like someone sucking the life out of me with a straw. They wanted us to go to the stage to nail our papers to the cross. The true concept of letting go. My nerves were all over the place, as each young lady moved to the stage to nail their papers. I waited for my time, but God had to tell me. I asked God to tell me when I needed to move and with quickness; I felt a soft touch and wind. We were in a building, but I could still feel His touch. Like I was outside in a field and the wind was blowing just for me.

With the heaviness of my heart, spirit, and body, I walked to the stage. Feeling the weight of the world and in a flash, I could see Jesus walking with his cross. It was hard, but I watched with my spirit. I saw it as Him rooting me on to get to that cross. Still thinking I couldn't do this, but Jesus reminded me I could. Looking at the paper with the names and other issues that I carried and got to the cross. They gave me the nail and the hammer and I remember leaning over it and nailing it to the cross. Usually, I was ashamed of what I did, but I heard a voice saying shout it out, so I did. I shouted my wrongs and my pain for all to hear as I nailed it to the cross. I hit the floor on my knees as I felt like I was having an out-of-body moment. When I got up, I felt free and I felt a release. This was the lightest I've felt in so long. I didn't know how much weight I was carrying until this moment. I felt reborn and a whole new person. Taking new breaths when a woman touched me and spoke so beautifully, I felt like she read my soul. Her face was well rounded as it was a perfect circle. Her eyes were small with an eyelid that looked like they were a garage door to the eye. She helped me up and as she did, I put all my weight onto her as I was weak. A strong woman she was because she just pulled dead weight off the floor. She was very gentle in her words and her touch but had a southern accent that I love to hear. It reminded me of home just like she reminded me of an angel that came from out of nowhere. This beautiful soul reminded me to be free and to forgive with my heart and not my mind. The most powerful statement I still hold on to. She explained to me that what I had just experienced was a release of the old me, but now it's time for the next step, which is true forgiveness.

The last thing she told me shook me because I knew no one knows what was on that paper as far as the issues.

"You have other issues you need to handle. Forgiveness was the step to really being free and healed. Do you want to be healed? It's time to prep yourself for birthing. What you about to birth will be greatness, but you have to forgive and be free to obtain it."

She read me like an open book and that made me nervous because that was nothing but God. I had other issues that were in front of me that were personal and were at home. The issues that I carried with those that are closed to me needed to be handled. This was going to take a real sit down with some past issues. I know what I needed to do, but honestly, sit-downs were something that I feared with people. Conflicts and I didn't match well together. I shut down with the quickness and taking the bait of being the one in the wrong. Being a yes girl, and that is how I made my moves. It was easier to take it than not. It's time to get over the fear if I want to move on. Now that I have covered the souls that I was attached to because of sex, it was time to deal with the souls that kept me angry, hurt, and always feeling like I wasn't wanted by the very people who birthed and raised me. In my heart, this step was hard, but I needed to deal with this and with the person from who I felt the most pain. My Mother..........

"For God so loved the world, that He gave His only begotten Son, that whosoever believeth in him should not perish, but have everlasting life."

John 3:16 KJV

Chapter Fifteen

Closed Womb Mother

Never too old to be free

Shatoria C

Friday, July 31, 2010, I became a wife and a mother all in one day. By August 2011, I was informed that I would never give birth to my own. When I said I do to Jerone, who I call "hubby", I gained an entire household that day. After all, I've been through, I couldn't believe that I had this title of wife and mother. I loved my family and all that was coming with it, except the fact of trying to have a baby of my own. Trying to become free of the things I was holding, part of that was anger. Along with my spiritual battle, I had a battle with my physical body. This battle started in 2010, and I became furious and bitter within myself. My heart was broken because this wasn't what I signed up for. I thought getting pregnant was going to be easy, but that wasn't my case. At the time I saw a test with scars, but God saw my faith and knew this battle was a testimony He was preparing for the world to hear and read.

Going to that conference and nailing everything in my heart to the cross was a huge relief. One of the biggest things I put on the paper when I nailed it to the cross, was my anger towards God about being a mom. I've hit many milestones in my life, but being a mom was a milestone I sought-out for in my heart. I was a wife, and that was a dream come true, but being a mother was such a passion for me. It burned in me like wood in a fireplace during the wintertime. God was adjusting me for marriage and being a mom, but I didn't prepare for the walk that I had to walk to get to each of those milestones. Hubby came into the relationship with my bonus son, who became the apple of my eye from the first day I placed eyes on him. I grew up in a blended family, so this was an easy move for me.

So, to back it up a bit, In August 2011 I found out I had a closed womb back. Over time I had many surgeries to repair my womb and they weren't working. My doctor who was working with me was outstanding and she worked to keep the faith with me. Over time of dealing with the infertility issue, I became depressed. It was becoming coming hard every month as each test would come back negative. I was tired of trying, praying, and hoping. I needed a break and needed it soon. Before the end of the conference, I could speak to the woman who helped me up, and we chatted a bit. She didn't know me before this, but she knew a lot about me. She started to describe the concept of a toxic womb. However, she didn't know me from Adam, so I understood this was from God. As she went on, she spoke about stresses and other things that can cause a lot of it. She looked me right in my eye and said unforgiveness is one of the biggest dangers to faith. She could read me and she did it well because she outright asked me about my mother.

We spoke about my mother and my past. I gave her everything I could. She had a look of grace over her and she held my hand as I spoke every word and detail. After about 15 minutes, she gave me a southern old school laugh, and we both started laughing. As she held my hand, she gave me a forgiving tap and explained some things about being a parent. She explained how being a mom doesn't start when that baby is born but within the heart of the mother. Just like giving birth, going through adoption, or however, a person becomes a mother it is not easy. Raising a child does not come with a how-to guide. My thoughts matched her words. I had to tell myself that you either trust God or you trust nothing. As a mother, you will have those decisions that are hard to make, but you have to do it. She asked me to think of my mother, our past, and her guidance on how to raise me. Reminding me that life isn't easy, but given the chance, people can change. She asked me to think about me being a mom to my bonus son, Jamorian, and think of the guidance I have had to raise him.

Being a mom for a short period, I have learned so much from my son. He showed me that parents don't have a manual and we are learning every day. I was learning how to understand that he has feelings, and he needed to know that I was there for him. But I also knew that there were things as parents that we go through that kids don't understand I learned that this job, along with my growth spiritually, my mom didn't know how to do what I needed and wasn't equipped for it either. She called every day and some days I didn't pick up and some days I did. I felt moments of no connection and that is really on me because I haven't forgiven her. I learned by listening and praying that this was her way of saying I'm sorry. With her call every day, I knew that she was ready to chat, and she wants to be a part of whatever I'm going through and my life. It was time to let her in and to be honest with her. She needed to know the truth. The truth of everything, even if it was going to hurt her feelings. We teach our kids to be open with us. Even though I am an adult, that little girl needed to be at rest and peace for once in her life.

As we kept with the conversation, she told me to not fear my closed womb as it was open and will birth greatness. But in the meantime, she wanted to know about my thoughts of my future in faith, family, and work. I included in our conversation about my move that I was about to make to Washington, D.C., and my business as an event planner. She said the smile that I had as I spoke about my desires and plans showed her that my heart was good and there is so much life within me. I could feel God reminding me that He wasn't done with me or my family yet. This beautiful woman had so much faith and so much heart, and I thank God for that moment with her. As the day ended, I thank her for everything because I needed that type of conversation. That moment and conversation with her was everything for me and it fed my soul. But she wasn't done yet. She laid hands on my stomach and prayed her heart out. I know God heard her as my spirit surely did. She prayed for the healing of my heart and for me to forgive those that God has forgiven. Which is everyone! As I said my goodbye to her, she told me to make sure on my way to Washington, that I make sure I stop by my mother's home. She will be expecting me. She said with great boldness:

"It's time to have that conversation and lay it at Jesus's feet."

I felt in my heart I wasn't ready for that conversation. I also felt that all the issues and pain were real. Before this conference and meeting this angel, I had already been diagnosed with endometriosis, spent thousands of dollars on ovulation kits, pregnancy tests, and multiple procedures which included many medicines, I cried an entire ocean over three years. I wasn't ready to deal with a close or toxic womb, but I wanted the opportunity to birth a child. As I cried and dealt with all this, I learn through these events of my life and the conversation at the conference that I didn't trust God. I had more trust in the medicines than God. They weren't working, so my faith swung back and forth like I was on a swing. During that time, I missed what He was speaking to me, which was to trust Him fully.

One of many lessons that I learned that He would not bless me until I handle my issues with my forgiveness. Yes, I knew I could be blessed in a storm, but not in a mess. I wouldn't treat the blessing right if I get it the way I desire to receive it. God had other plans, and I had to learn my plans weren't what He wanted. God was laughing at my plans. After a while, I had to laugh too, because I was trying to tell God what to do and how to handle my blessing. I had to find my rightful seat and sit down somewhere and learn to respect God's flow. That moment was coming as I saw His work unfold.

I wrote down my travel plans for my move to Washington and part of that was going to visit Georgia. I prepared for the drive from Oklahoma to Georgia and then on to D.C. I intended to go home, see family, and get to our new home. No one knew my plans of trying to have a baby or even having a conversation with my mother. I needed to pray about this conversation and pray about just being back to a place I don't like and didn't feel comfortable with. The only thing that stood in between me and speaking to my mother was my nerves and the 12-hour drive that was ahead of me. Our conversation needed to be face to face, and I had to be upfront and honest. Even if she doesn't like what I was saying.

I've been home before, but my feelings were all over the place and I was nervous. I didn't feel comfortable with myself. Spirits were strong here and I can't cave into them. One thing about me is that I'm a punk and don't want to have conversations. My communication is the worst, and I don't know how to deal with issues without being that little girl. The little girl who has always been afraid to speak up for herself, the one that felt that I was a disappointment to others, is now thinking about sitting and talking with her mother. The questions… was my mother ready for this sit-down. I felt sick to my stomach and very overwhelmed with what I needed to do. With the drive ahead of me, I had a lot of praying I needed to do and I needed that time to get my nerves together. As I prepared for this trip, I realized that there was so much I didn't know about my mom. I think because when I was younger, I couldn't see past the drugs, hurt, and neglect. Even after she got clean and got her life together, our relationship was still toxic. I didn't trust her and couldn't count on her. Now, as an adult, I know I didn't leave room to accept her and who she had become. I read her diary when I was about 16 and she knew my feelings about her, my heart towards her, and my pain. I remember telling her I didn't want to spend the weekends with her and I saw the hurt in her eyes. But I didn't know that she was trying. Truly, I didn't care if she was trying. I wasn't into loving and forgiveness at that time. My mind was hurt and broken. The heart was damaged, torn into tiny pieces, and looked like it was put through a shredder. My mind went into the conversation and how it was going to work. I was about to have a real sit down about who my mom was, as she wasn't the mom I remembered when I was left at the age of ten.

During this drive, I played out the conversation over and over in my head. Those thoughts came to a stop when I got to Georgia. I was only going to be home for two days, which was the day I got there and the next day. I wanted to see everyone and enjoy spending time with friends and family. As nightfall soon arrived, I know I needed a good night's sleep. My mind was all over the place as I was laying down and I couldn't sleep well. I remember asking God to give me peace. My mind was spinning like a ball on a finger and I just wanted to rest. God started to come to me clearly as I closed my eyes and I started to listen. His words seemed to be the only voice in the room. I took a deep breath in and slowly out and as He spoke, I felt peace.

He told me to stop creating more storms in my path as they are destructive and distracting me. Nothing I was facing was new to Him, and I was being equipped for the things planned for me. I needed to remember to trust Him with all of my faith and depend on Him with everything. He continued to speak. He also told me to be ready for my change, as they will see someone different because I am not the same spiritually or physically. There was work He was doing in me and I would soon understand. The change that we're approaching would be quick and that He will provide beauty instead of ashes. I didn't know what that meant at that moment, but I was going to find out soon. Not remembering much of anything after this, but waking up from a good sleep. I woke up in a great space and my nerves wasn't so bad. Didn't want to surprise her so, I called my mom to let her know I was coming by for a visit. She sounded so excited and ready. I've been praying that I was ready and praying that this conversation went well. It was time for me to meet the spiritual side of my mother. I know that I have changed, but I now understand that she has changed as well. Not meeting the person who I felt I have disliked for years. Today was going to be a brand-new day, and I was going in with the knowledge, peace, and faith that things had already changed.

"And He Changeth the times and the seasons: he removeth kings, and setteth up kings: he giveth wisdom unto the wise, and knowledge to them that know understanding"

Daniel 2:21 KJV

Chapter Sixteen

Mother to Mom

"With Christ I am guided and not with my emotions."

Shatoria C

Sitting outside of my mother's home gave me chills. This home my mother and step-father have had for years. The house was in a peaceful neighborhood, but what I hated about the house was that it sat on the downslope of a hill. Trying to drive up and down that hill was a headache, and even walking the hill made your legs hurt. Many trees surrounded the house as if she lived in the woods. I don't enjoy living near trees or ponds to this day. Another reason is that sometimes stray animals and snakes used to pop up out of the blue. Used to scare the mess out of me. Mostly at night because there were no street lights on this road either. They built the home out of different sizes of brown-colored bricks. I stared at the house more and it looked damaged. It looked like what I have felt for years. Broken and unfixable and wanting to be whole. Looking at the house, my memories flowed of the things that they said over the years. I used to hate coming to this house, but things change. Coming out of my daydream and remembered why I was there. This wasn't just a visit, but things I need to get off my chest, and a moment of truth. I sat in my car and looked around the yard and the front of the home. Attempting to get my nerves in check so I can get out of the car and walk into the house. I was nervous for many reasons because being upfront and confronting my issues was about to be center stage. I finally got the nerves to get out of my way and get out of the car.

I walked up the long walkway to the door of the house with my son, nieces, and nephew in tow and I saw that mom still had the Air Force Proud Mom on the door. I put that there before I left to go into the military all those years ago. Getting to the front door, I was clear in my mind and felt a sense of love as I saw my mother sitting at her computer. She gave me the biggest smile, and I was feeling a peacefulness that I've never felt before. I walked into the house to all the familiar things. My mother wasn't the mother physically from what I described before. Over time, her life changed, so did mine. She had a stroke my senior year of high school. Because of her stroke, her appearance was different. A piece of her skull was missing, which caused a dent on the right side of her head. She had gained weight and wheelchair-bound. Being paralyzed on her left side, after her stroke, which affected everything from walking and talking. She walked sometimes, with a cane and a brace on her leg. That didn't stop her from beaming with happiness when I saw her. She smiled so much and her words were different along with her tone when she spoke. Seeing me, her eyes beamed like a shining star in the sky. There was such joy in her eyes, which made it easy for me to go through the door to the next step.

The kids all came in and gave their love to their grandmother and made themselves comfortable with the television. As the kids played and hung out, mom offered them candy and they not going to say no. They were at their grandparent's house. There were no rules here. Speaking to my son, and they laughed a bit. She adored him, and that was something that blessed my heart. He got a surprise as she had a present for him, which was a GameStop gift card because he loved that place. They had that in common, playing games. She played on her computer and he played on his game station. I hugged her, and she spoke to me with her slow speech. Just another effect of the stroke. I admired her at this moment because she had such peace about her and she didn't look the same. Her description, in the beginning, wasn't what I saw in front of me. With drugs, abuse, and years of pain, she had aged a bit. She was just 52 years old, but she looked older than that. All those things had taken a toll on her, but she was living to see another day and I was glad to see she was in good spirits. Her peace was something I haven't felt for myself, and I wanted that feeling. I sat down next to her on the floor and we started chatting. Finally, the small talk turned into the actual conversation and the deep dive that I needed.

This moment was mine and mine alone. I remember this conversation or should I say, her words to me. It still lives with me in the moments I think of her. When she spoke, her words were full of sorrow and pain, but I felt her heart. She let her heart all out that day, and all I could do was hang on to each word. I wasn't ready as she came out the gate with some dreams she was having. Explaining to me she was having dreams of me being pregnant. Just a few of my closest friends knew I was trying. I hadn't explained or talked to my mother or grandmother about it. She ended up asking me if I was pregnant and my face told my truth. She laughed as she reminded me of how my face would give me away. She was right, and to this day I'm still working on it. I didn't want to give details yet of what was going on, and as I was thinking of the next thing to say, she told me about her walk-in life trying to get pregnant. I sat there confused and surprised because I didn't know she had any issues. But today I was about to learn who my mother was. You know as a child when

someone asks you what your mother's name is and you say mom....
that was that feeling right there. I was about to learn my mother's
actual name, which was Veverly. Understand I knew my mother's
name, but I was about to learn who she was.

She looked over at the children playing and talking and gave a
smile. She started to explain how she had a miscarriage right before
she got pregnant with us. The doctors told her she would not have
any children. When she said she was pregnant nine times, my heart
went south. I felt like I was on a rollercoaster and it was going down
pretty fast. My ears became very eager to listen to her, but I was
listening to her heart as she kept talking. I had no words as she
explained each one of her pregnancies. She was deep in thought
when she spoke about it. I could see that she felt that pain again. She
never really found out why she would have a miscarriage before
each successful pregnancy, and that played a small part in the reason
she was so angry and so hard. She was dealing with the death of
her own children and as a woman, you question if you are even a
woman sometimes because of this.

I felt that for sure, as I was angry and hurt at everything and
everyone. Trying to have a family took a toll on her, and it took a toll
on me physically and mentally too. I finally looked her in her eyes
and she read me completely. I didn't have to tell her I understood
her walk. She looked at me like a proud parent and assured me that
all will be well and to keep my faith. At that moment, I believed
her as I felt her heart and her truth. She explained God understood
my pain what I was feeling, and she knew it was deeper for me. I

got the nerves to explain to her what the doctors were telling me. I explained I was feeling like she felt. I was feeling like I was alone and abandoned because I didn't know what to expect or how to expect to deal with infertility.

When I said the word infertility her position changed and she tells me about her past and why she did, said, and felt the things she did. I won't tell that story as that isn't mine to tell, but she had a lot of pain. She explained some of her actions towards me. She felt our relationship was broken and I was better off where I was and now as an adult, I think so as well. Admitting she didn't treat me right, and there was no excuse for it, but we couldn't change the past. Speaking about her pain she endured through her relationships and how they derailed things for her. These were a few reasons why she never gave me the sex talk, or how she wasn't able to guide me in anything. I now understood that she couldn't be a mother because she didn't know how to be one. It all made sense. Next out of her mouth shocked my very being. She said she was sorry for not protecting me. Protecting me from people and things as I was growing up. I took that and understood it fully. The mistakes were great, but they were forgivable, and so was she.

I finally was open with some things as we are being open. Getting my nerves up, I explained that there was so much I hated about life growing up. Explaining to her how I hated her male friends and how she picked them over me. I was young and trying to get through life. She looked me in my face and her eyes met mine. She asked me to go on and I told her the biggest thing I hated was being touched. Her eyes increased with water and she turned her head. Her face seemed intense as the soul left her. I knew that hurt her and that wasn't my intention at all, but it was freeing us both. She whispered under her breath, "I knew it." I asked her, did she really want to know? She looked at me and said she needed to know. I didn't go into grave details, but I gave her enough that she shook her hand and waved her hand for me to stop. Her leg shakes and she put her fist under her chin and looked at the computer. I felt at that moment that I messed up and did I need to tell her what happened. Was she ready for what I was saying? Could she deal with it? My thoughts were all over the place and I asked God to please step in as I was feeling uncomfortable. God didn't waste any time. My mother cleared her throat and her next comment set me fully free.

"I can't explain or give you all the answers to what you want or what happened. I can't because I don't have them either. I made mistakes and I've made mistakes with how I handled you. I can't take it back and I'm sorry."

What I heard set me up to cry. My eyes watered up as it was the sorry that I needed. I held on to the tears because I didn't want the kids to see anything. The tears were not of pain, but freedom and joy. She asked me was I good? I shook my head yes and told her I am, and I said thank you for that. I needed that. She smiled, and I smiled with a slight laugh. We sat in silence for a few minutes until we got ourselves together. She looked at me and said the name of the Thief and I shook my head yes. She said she should have known that it was something about him and how he looked at us. But she thought it was all in her mind. I explained to her I have been healed from that and him. Feeling better as he was no longer on earth, but it wouldn't surprise me if he did that to other girls. My mother agreed with me. She was saying he would say things that didn't make sense, but her head wasn't in the game to clearly understand. Her gut said one thing, but with all that was on her plate, she didn't know how to react to her gut. I explained to her that it is okay because I know now that parenting isn't easy and I've learned that I have to be upfront about life and how I feel. He is no longer here and I have better days.

After a brief moment of silence, we moved the conversation over to marriage and life. Our conversation was deep but relaxing if that makes sense. I questioned God about my memories and why I had them. Many of them I didn't care for, but they were there. I needed to remember, so I didn't repeat my history. I felt such peace in our conversation, and I felt like I lost weight with it too. My heartfelt better because I could feel its healing. It felt so good and so right. The world looked, smelled, and sounded different. She didn't see me as a person but as her daughter; her baby girl, as she told me. That is what I needed. At that moment God reminded me of His promise that He would never leave me nor forsake me and He never lied.

We talked more about us trying to have a baby and what our plans were. I felt ready enough to tell her about IVF and the process. She was excited and said she will be supportive and was clear about being just that. It felt so good explaining to her everything and what we were about to embark on. She assured me she would be there every step of the way. I felt all the love and freedom that I didn't want to leave, but getting back on the road was a must. This drive gave me pleasure, knowing of the conversation I had early this year with the woman from the conference, and how all she said was confirmed and completed. I had my mother back, and just in time to walk this walk with me. What a walk it was. It was not an easy one. I was just happy to have my mother back in my life, and now I could take the next step. I didn't know all that was ahead of me, but I felt great not walking it alone or afraid anymore. All I knew at the moment was that things were right and I was free and at peace. We both were free that day and I gained her back in my life. Her title for me shifted from mother to mom. I got my mom back. She told me to be ready for a shift and I thought I was, but I wasn't ready for the shift that required me to say goodbye.

"For I know the thoughts that I think toward you, saith the Lord, thoughts of peace, and not of evil, to give you an expected end."

Jeremiah 29:11

Chapter Seventeen

Final Goodbye

"Always in my heart."

Shatoria C

August 5, 2013, I found out we were pregnant naturally and soon miscarried. Mom and grandmother were the first ones I called. They cried with me. I had both women as my backbone as I dealt with the unknown. They help me get through it, and yes; I had hubby and other families, but to have these two women made the pain a bit easier. When we started the IVF process, they both were there every step of the way. Mom kept having dreams of me being pregnant and I was trying to stay in faith with it as she was really in faith for us. Wednesday, November 13, 2013, we found out that we were expecting a baby. I was nervous about it all. Finding out we were expecting, I desire to shout it to the moon, but was nervous. What I needed was a mom, and she was just that, and I loved it. They instructed me to take it easy and, I knew I needed to, but then there was a shift in the plans of resting or thinking positive things.

I spoke to mom on Thanksgiving and even though the conversation seemed a bit off, I kept on with the conversation. We talked so much, I knew her tone and breaths and she didn't sound right. She stilled tried to speak, ended up rushing me off the phone. She said she will call me after she gets in from Black Friday shopping. I said okay, and we said we would talk tomorrow. I thought nothing of it until that Friday when my grandmother called. That Friday morning scared me as hubby was at work and I had the worst pain that it woke me up out of my sleep. I called hubby, and he got me and my nerves back on track. It scared me to where I needed to go back to sleep. I told myself I would call my mom and grandmother later when I woke up.

My grandmother called me and when I answered the phone like

I always do, her entire demeanor was different. Her hello to me was short and to the point. She asked me have I spoken to any of my sisters, and I said no and asked why? She explained that my mom was in the hospital and she would be fine. I asked the regular five W's because I liked to make sure I have all the facts. She didn't answer my questions, and I know my grandmother. She knew, but she didn't want to stress me out by telling me. At that moment I didn't care, I wanted to know. I felt I needed to know. My grandmother was stubborn and refused to tell me anything except she would keep me posted and mom is fine. I hung up the phone and cried because I know there is something wrong, but I didn't know what it was. After our conversation, I screamed for hubby to come up and see me as I was still in the bed resting. I tried to explain what was going on and he told me to calm down and it will be fine. He prayed over me to keep me at peace and let me know all would be well. I trusted him as he has always had me, but I felt like something wasn't right. I needed to be at peace. I was pregnant and I needed to be mindful of my stress because that morning; we had a scare. What I wasn't ready for was what the next eight weeks were about to bring forth.

The month of November became a blur and December became unnoticeable, but I had to be positive. Within four weeks I found out my mom had lung cancer, and it was spreading quickly. There was nothing they could do to help her. She went from stage three to four, to terminal in about four to five weeks. She couldn't speak, but she could hear. I would tell my stepfather things to tell her, and he would show her pictures of my ultrasounds of the baby Feeling like she was coming home and that was what I believed. Asking God for her healing and He said I got her. The change wasn't coming, but I was faithful in my thoughts. I went a long time saying I didn't need to see her. That was my mindset because I felt like I couldn't deal. In my feelings, hurt and mad about the situation my mom was in. We just got it together and were doing so well with each other. I was trying to stay in the word, but let me be honest, I'm human and my flesh wasn't hearing it. Needing my mom more than anything at those moments in my life. I couldn't talk to her and couldn't tell her what was going on. Aching for her voice, and honestly, our last conversation where I heard her voice was on Thanksgiving. She knew she had an issue, and she knew it was serious. When they told me she was terminal, I became angry on the inside. I stood firm that she was going to be healed and she was going to be great. In my heart and mind, she was good. I knew God was healing her. Nothing and no one was going to tell me any other way. The day my stepfather called me to say my mom wanted to see me, I knew something was up and I wasn't ready. I didn't want to see her in that state that she was in. Didn't think my heart could take it. After speaking with hubby and much prayer, I finally chose of going home to see her as God instructed me to. It was easy to not deal with it because I didn't live in Georgia anymore, so I didn't have to see the process that everyone else in the family was seeing. God had protection over me for many reasons because He knows how much I could handle.

I went home during a four-day weekend in January 2014. That

was one of the longest flights I've had, well that's how I felt. I prepared myself for the hospital. I was giving myself the biggest pep talk I could, and my bonus sister prayed with me and told me to be ready. That is what I needed to do, but I wasn't ready. I finally arrived at the hospital and parked the car. I felt like I was in the locker room about to hit that floor for a game as I was this scared little girl. Just like I prepped myself to talk to my mom back in April, I had to prep myself to walk through this hospital door. I got my bags and got out of the car. Walking through the hospital, I prayed, and out of nowhere, I get to the double doors where my mom was living out her days. I took a deep breath, and I walked towards the door and before I got there, a nurse asked me who I was, and who I was looking for. But she didn't finish because she said I looked just like my mother. She laughed a bit and said she was waiting for you. I walked up to the door and when they moved the curtain back, my heart dropped, but I kept smiling. I needed her to see me be strong because I could see her feelings all on her face. She was determined to look well and act it, and I was going to do the same.

I looked around the room, and she was hooked up to all these tubes and machines. She couldn't speak a word, but she could smile. It was a half-smile and as I watched her; I kept my tears back. I walked to her and gave her the biggest hug I could give her in that condition. Not seeing or being touched since her since April; her hug was warm. She had just celebrated another birthday, even though she was in the hospital. In my heart, I felt this would be temporary. We had plans for her to come to D.C. to help with the baby shower and stay for about a month to help me with the baby. I was excited that she wanted to come and be with me for that long, knowing she couldn't travel like that, but she was open and wanted to do it. I kept that memory in my head. She broke my train of thought when she waved me over to rub my pregnant belly, and she kept that smile. I grab a chair to get comfortable and spend the day with her. It felt awesome spending that time with her. I was there all day, but time went by so quickly. I got there about 11 that morning and it was almost nine when I left.

I only left because my mother and the nurse said I needed to rest. Since I was only 13 weeks pregnant, I thought I was good, but because I did IVF I looked further along, and yes, I was tired and I was considered high risk. Admitting she was right as I was physically and mentally weary and drained. I didn't want to leave her because, in my heart, I just got her back fully. This became the longest weekend of my life. A weekend I would never forget and that social media reminds me of too. As the weekend flowed, things happened that struck my nerves. I watched my mom get worse before my eyes. It was one of the hardest things to watch. At least I took a moment to see family and friends. My friends took me out to breathe and laugh a bit. It helped a little, but there was such a cloud over me because reality was in front of me and I wanted to stay in my dream. During my last days home, God showed me some things and had a proper conversation with me. I remember bits and pieces:

"Embrace this moment as I have prepared you for this. There is always a time and place, and there are seasons and reasons. I

make no mistakes, and this moment is purposely designed for right
now. Do not fear, as I have a plan and my plans are good. You,
my child, is covered and right now you don't understand, but you
will."

He was right that I didn't understand, but I knew in my heart that she wasn't coming home. It was like me sitting there watching her go through something and I can't help at all. I looked forward to the baby shower and her being there. Because of her stroke, she missed out on so much in my life, like my wedding and graduation from basic training. But all of that didn't matter at that moment. But I had it in my head, she would not miss anything else. I know how God is, and He is powerful, but at that moment, I wanted to see my mom walk out of that hospital. But truth be told, I knew when I asked for her to be healed; He was doing just that. Not the way we wanted it, but for a purpose that needed to be served. That has never left me and as I write this, I still feel it. I came to understand that she was leaving, but God was reminding me of her spirit. That she was healed right in front of us. We have to see it spiritually. See, God had to remind me of what he said back in April 2013, when He said I would see her differently. I needed to watch her spiritually, and not through the natural eye. He reminded me of her presence and that I needed to see her before the drugs and the stroke. Taking my eyes off of the right now moment and seeing her truly gave me chills. She was an awesome woman who had struggled, but what I saw right now was my mom being my mom even as she struggles with what she had in front of her.

Monday was the last day I was in town for this trip. By this time, cancer had spread and all they could do was make her comfortable. She knew when to ask me to be home to see her because she knew what was about to take place. That Monday evening, we spent some hours together, just me and her. We talked and laughed, but as the hour went by, the talking and laughing decreased. As her pain increased, I prayed for her, gave her gentle touches, and just told her how much I loved her. It felt so good. I knew in my spirit that this was the last time I would do this. Keeping with the smile for her and she told me I needed to go and get my rest. She mouthed how beautiful I was and how grown up I've become. Expressing how proud of me she was. Touching my stomach and asking do we have a name and what I thought we were having. I told her I know it is a girl even though we haven't had the appointment yet, and we wanted to name her Janae Ann. Ann being both her middle name and my mother-in-love middle's name. She giggled and kept rubbing my stomach. She looked and I could see the glitter in her eyes. It sparkled like a star and I couldn't help but stare. My mother said the most beautiful words to me I won't forget:

" I will watch her till she comes home. She will be fine."

It was more, but she was mouthing her words and in pain. I made out what she was trying to say. I kissed her hands and embraced her words. My heart filled with tears, but I wouldn't let them fall. Mom looked me in my face and so many words told me to let her go. All I could do was shake my head yes, and be okay with it. This was the last time I would see her alive, last time I would kiss her cheeks, last time for her touch, and the last time she would tell me she loved me. That broke my heart to pieces. I gave her the longest kiss I could give. She didn't say good night, but she did say goodbye. I told mom how I loved her and I always will. As I walked out, the nurse hugged me in the hallway. For me, that sealed it, and I knew for sure I wouldn't see her again. The nurses were remarkable. She told me that she would take care of my mom for me. The hug the nurse gave me said it was okay for me to cry, but before it got worse, I thanked her again; I walked to my car and cried like a baby. I cried so hard because I didn't know what to do or how to feel. I was hurting and I just wanted to go home. Real talk, I just wanted my mom.

It took me a long time to get home that Tuesday as the weather was bad with snow. Flights were delayed and diverted a couple of times. During that flight home, I had a lot of thoughts of why my child that I'm carrying won't meet her grandmother? Why mom has to die? I went home and went back to work trying to stay focus. Everything about my feelings and what I was thinking had me questioning all my feelings. People were wondering why I was at work and what I was doing. They even question how I was grieving. I just needed positive people in my life at that moment. I remember the call from my stepfather that following Monday about planning her service. I was strong on the phone, but crying is something I was trying not to do. My mom leaving me was becoming reality and I wish I could wake up.

Wednesday, January 29, 2014, at 7:20 in the morning at 15 weeks pregnant, I lost my mom even though I gained an angel. That pain hurt like hell. I felt like someone stabbed me in my heart and was turning the knife. Being hurt, mad, and angry, and even though we knew it was coming, I felt I wasn't ready. My heart was so crushed and yes, I questioned God, and He reminded me of everything has a reason, season, and purpose. I accepted that, but at that moment that was the hardest of them all to accept and take in. I never knew how hard it would be to say goodbye, but I did, and that was a goodbye that will forever live with me.

What I will remember is from April 2013 to January 2014, I was able to have my mom. A woman is pregnant for nine months and nine months my mom loved me as if I was in her womb again. Even though we weren't near each other, it was like the umbilical cord linked us spiritually. The bond was wholesome and beautiful. I cherish those nine months and I will always know the importance of them. My heart and my boo bear, I will never forget our final goodbye but our love is for a lifetime.

Veverly A. North

4 January 1961 - 29 January 2014

"There are good women, but you are the best. Grace and beauty can fool you, but a woman who respects the Lord should be praised. Give her the reward she deserves. Praise her in public for what she had done."

Proverbs 31:29-31

Chapter Eighteen

Birthing Forgiveness

New life brings in new lights

Shatoria C

Carrying a child and dealing with death at the same time caused me great pain trying to find the proper way of grieving. As months went by, I remained in a very dark space. Work was going left, and I was trying to understand why God allowed this to happen. I just wanted my mom, but I couldn't be selfish with it. My heart wanted what the heart wanted, and that was my mom. I struggled for months, trying to figure out my place and getting through the moments that should be important. I didn't do maternity photos and I let myself go physically, mentally, and spiritually. Things on television and things around me kept me bound in my heart and mind. Mother's Day came, and it was a blur. I hated that day and didn't want to celebrate it. Even though hubby worked hard to do so. I felt the movement of my child and kept counting every movement as it scares me. I didn't want to lose anyone else in my life. As the date to the baby shower got close, I had anxiety that came in full force. I thought I was coping, but I wasn't. I stayed busy as a way not to feel or think. I thought this would work. I needed peace, and it wasn't coming fast enough.

The morning of the shower I was in a deep sleep and this dream, I could feel the most beautiful wind. This was the event my mother was supposed to be a part of, and in this dream was the most beautiful presence of peace I could have found from the world itself. In this dream, I had a great conversation with my mother as I was longing for her for weeks. God knew what I needed, but there was more to it. The dream felt so real, even though I know it wasn't. In this dream, I got to see my mom. The younger mom didn't have a brace or any signs of a stroke. She gave me a hug and the gentlest kiss. We sat down and I remember wanting to cry and she told me no tears. Explaining how she was fine and was at peace and speaking the same words as God and that there are reasons, season, and a purpose. She served her time and did what she was called to do. I didn't know what that was at that moment, and she reminded me that her purpose in life has been filled. She told me to stop worrying and enjoy the moments of being pregnant. To not allow her death to take away my joy, but to add laughter in the place of my pain. I was hurting because I wanted my mom here with me physically. She loved me and reminded me she is there and hasn't left me. She laughed and rubbed my belly and said the birth of forgiveness is beautiful.

Her words to me in this dream caused me to think on a whole different level. I remember pieces as I wrote what I can remember down:

"You needed to be free of things to be able to carry the gift that you are blessed with. God can't grow a seed in a toxic space because it is not getting the light, water, and love it needs when it is blocked by darkness, hatred, and unforgiveness. Be completely free of self-guilt, my death is not your fault. Be free of being ashamed completely, you have grown from those things that you thought you were, and let go of the things you didn't understand, they will be seen shortly. God has forgiven you already, so don't keep wondering if He has. It's done."

I didn't want the dream to end. I wanted to stay with her for that whole moment, but I knew it was going to end and it needed to. It ended with her kissing me and telling me she is still with me. She hasn't missed any of the great moments and she loves me. My mom told me to trust myself with my heart and follow God's advice and trust Him, as I would need all of Him and His hands. The rain would come, but to remember that the rainbow would always follow. I stood with that, and I felt the baby was our rainbow after the storm. She also informed me that she will be there for the birth as I am being prepared for such a great moment. She kissed me again for the absolute last time. I wanted to stay with her. She told me it was time to go, and she is with me. Noticing our distance starting to grow more apart; I saw this beautiful light. It seemed like she was floating away and my tears grew as she disappeared from my sight

I woke up, and I cried my eyes out. Grabbing my pillow and squeezed it to scream because I didn't want anyone to hear me. Got to get through this day and get me together. My emotions were high and I put on my mask of smiles to get through the day. It was a beautiful Saturday in June, and the time with friends and family was beautiful. Seeing everyone was nice and time well spent. Watching everyone together, felt like I was in my dream. I had a very personal moment where I felt the wind again. When I notice my feelings were catching up with me again, I worked to keep them in check because I didn't want anyone to know how I felt. I took a walk away from the crowd as we were outside by the water. That wind was telling me that all is well and that mom was there. It helped me enjoy the rest of my day with everyone. After that beautiful day and dream came to an end, I was still taking it day by day. I kept reminding myself that I could do this.

My mom's death gave me true meaning to living and knowing that there is more to life than death. I learned I was pregnant with God's plan. He knew I would go through all of this before I was formed in my mom's womb. This baby that I carried was the gift of my forgiveness and trusting God. My goal was trying to stay afloat with my feelings and work to not stress myself out over things I didn't have control over. As my due date came closer, my fear grew. I didn't know what I was getting into as a parent, but I was finding out sooner than later. All the plans I had for the birth of my daughter went right out the window, God had plans beyond my reach.

12 days after that dream with my mom, I birth someone beyond my dreams and one of the biggest blessings of my life. Thursday, June 19, 2014, at 4:14 pm, Janae Ann graced us with her presence in a Godly type of form. When I met this baby, I saw my mom and the things my mom told me. I remember she said she isn't missing anything, so I knew she was there. Giving birth showed me that God is true to His word. Everything I prayed for and desired when it came down to being a mom was right in front of me. I was looking and holding a piece of forgiveness and I have to say; I have never felt so at peace and honor for such a gift. Birthing forgiveness and the meaning are; I could open myself up to forgive those who have hurt and harmed me over the years. Being able to walk in love, which it allowed God to do the work He had for me. I didn't know that the

journey would be me letting things go.

Many will say how can you forgive someone who has done such bad things to you and against you? How could you just let it go? Many say they can't do it or won't and you know what I'm okay with how they feel. But for me, I got tired of having a toxic womb. I didn't know what my forgiveness would do for me or too me, but it was the biggest blessing I could have ever done. Letting go and letting God be the one to deal with those that have hurt me. There is nothing I could do to get back at those who have hurt me but forgive them. This hurts them more than anything because I have moved on and I have healed from that type of pain. That pain kept me bound and locked up. I was missing blessings and I couldn't afford to miss anymore. I just birth someone who came from me forgiving the very person who has hurt me but looks at how God healed us just off of the fact we let go and let Him do what he does. That was the biggest blessings of it all. Birthing something greater than myself is priceless and beautiful.

"The Son paid the price to make us free. In him we have forgiveness of our sins"

Colossians 1:14 KJV

Chapter Nineteen

Being My Authentic Self

"Loving me. Forgiving me."

Shatoria C

What if my foundation was never formed? What if I've never experienced a child's fear? What if I've never sung fear not? What if I've fought my fears at seven? What if I've said no? What if I've never left McDaniel Street? What if I've never left the city to go to the country? New everything, is it really? What if I've never release? What if I don't get over many encounters? What if I've never went through the thirty-day shift? What about if I never had my great escape? What if I've never stepped from death? What if I never had soul tied to my soul. What if I wasn't a close womb mother. What if she never went from mother to mom? What if I had never said my final goodbye? What if I've never birth forgiveness? What if I didn't be my authentic self? What if??

If I have never gone through all of the above, then I wouldn't be able to tell you my story. Every chapter in this book has been part of my road map to life. I don't regret anything and I'm not ashamed of anything that is written. You should look over the chapters in your life. Your life chapters may seem dark, but there are lights at the end of the tunnels. I didn't see them at first and I almost gave up, but I'm glad I didn't. Starting with forgiving myself and freeing myself from all the things that held me in chains. Freedom is beautiful to the soul and the mind. I was free to love myself and was released from past issues. To free then to love to be me. I learned that my mom didn't leave me in vain. Her name rings within me all the time. What remains the same is that I am my mother's child, as I do have many ways of her. Working to better myself and do better in life. Mom taught me a lot, but the biggest lesson outside of forgiveness was that I should always be transparent to myself and others.

Learning to be my authentic self has been what has kept me moving. The saying that truth sets you free is a real statement, as I have spoken my truth with no shame. Staying the course has allowed me to be mindful of who I am and what I am called to do, no matter what others may say, think, or feel of me. I'm sure many will talk about me because of what I have put in this book, but at the end of it all, I'm free from it. No matter how people may feel about me, I've learned to be confident in myself and to cheer myself on. My assignment is to be positive and walk with people, as this isn't easy and life is short. My goal in life is to be what God has called me to be and do what He has instructed. He allowed me to see my mom as an example for walking in love, loving your past, and living for the future. As we all have a past, the thing I want you to take from this is that we are forgiven.

I Love me. All of me.

I adore myself. All of myself.

I am beautiful. Every part of me.

I give myself grace. Because I deserve it.

You are not a mistake. Here for a purpose.

You are a gift. You are priceless.

You are powerful. Strong in many forms.

You are worthy. Remember the passion you hold.

I will be myself and I will always be authentic and transparent to myself!

"In Christ we are made free by His blood sacrifice. We have forgiveness of sins because of God's rich grace"

Ephesians 1:7

ABOUT THE AUTHOR

Shatoria L. Christian was born on November 3, 1982. She is the wife to Jerone and a mom to two kids, Jamorian and Janae. While writing, she used her voice for issues that have played major roles in her life. Those issues are what helped to write this book. Shatoria wears many hats that include being a sister, an aunt, a mentor, a friend, and a believer in faith. She graduated from Columbia Southern University, with a bachelor's degree in business in 2019. Shatoria is currently working on a Master's of Business degree at American Military University.

In addition to writing, she currently serves as the voice and creator of the I Am Shatoria Podcast and brand. A podcast that allows people to voice their issues and a place where affirmation, love, forgiveness, and a whole lot of faith are shared.

Website: Iamshatoria.com

Podcast: Iamshatoria.podbean.com

Email: Shatoria@iamshatoria.com

CPSIA information can be obtained
at www.ICGtesting.com
Printed in the USA
BVHW052333120821
614281BV00012B/440

9 781637 902035